I0445380

MARTIN LUTHER'S
Little Intruction Book

A Classic Treasury of Timeless Wisdom and Reflection

Martin Luther's Little Instruction Book
ISBN: 979-8-88898-177-1 - *Paperback*
ISBN: 979-8-88898-178-8 - *Hardcover*
ISBN: 979-8-88898-179-5 - *Ebook*
Copyright © 2026 by Honor Books, Racine, WI

Martin Luther:

MAN OF FAITH, MAN OF CONVICTION

O ver five hundred years ago, a German monk and professor of theology named Martin Luther (1483-1546) quietly challenged the widespread practice of buying your way into heaven through the purchase of indulgences. (*An indulgence was being forgiven and absolved of any punishment for a sin from a church representative.*) His motivation came from the biblical truth that to inherit eternal life with God, "the just shall live by faith." Little did he realize his teachings would begin the largest Christian movement in the world-Protestantism.

Before coming to this understanding, Luther had remained perplexed by his inability to be holy enough for God to love. This drove him to a an in-depth study of the Bible, where he discovered that only the work of Jesus Christ on the cross paid the price for his sins. He realized that only through faith in Jesus as his Lord and Savior would he become a child of God, a true Christian. Rather than trusting in his good deeds, he simply believed in Jesus and received eternal life.

Luther's revelation of the grace of God, which opposed the manmade religious traditions of his time, has left an undeniable mark on our civilization. Known as the father of the Reformation, Martin Luther was a multi-faceted character who could be both tenderhearted and generous, as well as confrontational and feisty. He greatly enjoyed God's earthly pleasures—food and drink, music and humor—and after being a monk he particularly appreciated married life.

In his engaging style, Luther addressed many issues that are strikingly relevant today. The selections in this small volume give you a sample of his wit and wisdom and the simple humanness of a man who knew he was loved by God.

Note: All quotes are from Martin Luther unless indicated otherwise.

YES AND AMEN

"Faith is the 'yes' of the heart, a conviction on which one stakes one's life."

The writer of Hebrews exhorts us to be unswerving in our faith. These are words Martin Luther lived by example. His conviction for the truth of the unconditional love of Jesus to be known by everyone brought him before powerful men, some of whom wanted him burned for it.

In this modern age, there are so many voices professing their own ways that it can make it easy for the straight and narrow path ahead of you to begin to appear winding. Cling to Christ, allow Him to wash you with His Word in your study, and keep a tender ear open to the Holy Spirit, who will guide you in living out your convictions with certainty and courage.

Let us hold unswervingly to the hope we profess, for he who promised is faithful.

HEBREWS 10:23 NIV

DID YOU KNOW

Luther was threatened with excommunication by Pope Leo X if he did not recant a long list of statements picked from his writings.
He refused, and was excommunicated in 1521–a ruling that the Catholic Church never lifted.

THE KEY TO HIS CONVERSION

"When by the Spirit of God, I understood these words, 'The just shall live by faith,' I felt born again like a new man. I entered through the open doors into the very Paradise of God!"

Every morning we wake up to a new day, our nature as humans to create habits and routines can often create the illusion we know exactly what it has to offer. You likely have a grumbling stomach to fill, a set of teeth that need brushing, a job to go to, a child to care for, some traffic to endure, etc.

However our lives are full of unknown factors that fill the space between point A and point B, some of which can alter how we get there, when we get there, or if we get there at all. Anyone that has experienced loss will tell you that tomorrow is not guaranteed. As Christians, instead of living in fear of the unknown, we are called to live by faith.

Find freedom from anxiety, worry, and fear—walk by faith today that God works everything together for the good of those who love Him.

"... the just shall live by faith."

ROMANS 1:17

BELIEVING THOUGH NOT SEEING

"[It is] astounding that I should believe him to be the Son of God who is suspended on the cross, whom I have never seen, with whom I have never become acquainted."

The miracle of faith is *"... confidence in what we hope for and assurance about what we do not see."* (Heb. 11:1) There are many beliefs that require a certain level of faith. A rock climber has faith in the manufacturing of their ropes and the strength of their knots when they ascend great heights. You have faith that you are made of atoms, even though you have likely never peered into a microscope at the tiny cells that make up your skin.

Our faith runs deeper than skin. It is our spirit's longing to see the glory of God manifested in this life and in the next. Celebrate this wonderful mystery today.

"Whom having not seen, ye love;
in whom, though now ye see him not,
yet believing, ye rejoice with joy
unspeakable and full of glory."

1 PETER 1:8

DID YOU KNOW

Legend has it that while Luther was travelling to law
school on horseback during a storm, he was nearly
struck by lightning. He was terrified and cried out to
God for help, promising he would become a monk in
return.

FAITH COMES FROM GOD

"Your faith comes from Him, not from you.
And everything that works faith within you comes from Him
and not from you."

Our faith is a mystery and it is a certainty. It is a gift from our Creator, who knit us together in our mother's wombs, woven into the very threads of our being. Long before we could speak His name, He had already spoken His love over us. This ancient faith connects us to the great cloud of witnesses—centuries of brothers and sisters who clung to the same promises, prayed the same prayers, and stood on the same Rock. Their stories remind us that faith is not something we manufacture, but it is something God awakens within us.

Our faith is also a delight to God, growing up from the seed He Himself has planted in every heart. When we trust Him we are responding to His quiet invitation inherent in us. Pause and delight in the beauty of it all: the mystery, the lineage, the hope, and the God who sustains it.

For it is by grace you have been saved, through faith—and this is not from yourselves, it is the gift of God—not by works, so that no one can boast.

EPHESIANS 2:8-9 NIV

MAKING SOMETHING
OUT OF NOTHING

"God creates out of nothing. Therefore, until a man is nothing, God can make nothing out of him."

T hroughout His life, Jesus repeatedly reminded his followers that He only does what He sees the Father doing—that apart from the Father, He can do nothing. Jesus's life was one of radical servanthood. The concept of the King of Kings, Creator of the universe, coming down to earth and washing the feet of fishermen ignites an almost offensive reaction as it did in Peter. And yet, our Lord says, *". . . the Son of Man did not come to be served, but to serve . . ."* (Matt. 20:28).

Humility and holiness were the essence of Jesus's conduct on earth, and the means by which we have been saved. Consider these words today:

"Take my yoke upon you and learn from me, for I am gentle and humble in heart, and you will find rest for your souls." (Matt. 11:29)

Have you approached the canvas of life with a desire to make your mark? Or perhaps you've been staring at a blank page for fear of making a mistake. Humbly allow the master Artist to guide your brushstrokes and teach you the way of a beautiful life.

Humble yourselves before the Lord,
and he will lift you up.

JAMES 4:10 NIV

PREACHING TO THE
MAIDS AND BABES

*"When I preach I regard neither doctors nor magistrates,
of whom I have above forty in my congregation; I have all my
eyes on the servant maids and on the children.
And if the learned men are not well pleased with that they
hear, well, the door is open."*

Though intellect is a gift and education is a great accomplishment, these things do not lift or lower our position before God. God is not impressed by diplomas and titles. What amazed Jesus was child-like faith and willingness to believe in a radically good God. Reflect on the story of the centurion:

> *". . . a centurion came to him, asking for help.
> "Lord," he said, "my servant lies at home paralyzed,
> suffering terribly." Jesus said to him, "Shall I come
> and heal him?" The centurion replied, ". . . just say
> the word, and my servant will be healed . . ." When
> Jesus heard this, he was amazed and said to those*

following him, "Truly I tell you, I have not found anyone in Israel with such great faith . . . Go! Let it be done just as you believed it would."

(Matt. 8:5-8, 10-11, 13)

Jesus said, "Let the little children come to me, and do not hinder them, for the kingdom of heaven belongs to such as these."

MATTHEW 19:14 NIV

BEGIN WHEN YOU'RE YOUNG

"When I was young, I read the Bible over and over and over again, and was so perfectly acquainted with it, that I could, in an instant, have pointed to any verse that might have been mentioned."

Many Christians lose their way adopting new doctrines or culture perpetuated by leaders which aren't rooted in God's word. Many children raised in the church are leaving, feeling shamed for asking questions that challenge their leaders and unequipped to search out answers for themselves. Martin Luther's life was threatened because of his desire for truth and the undiluted Word of God over human tradition and authority.

Proverbs 22:6 says, *"Train up a child in the way he should go: and when he is old, he will not depart from it."* Teaching by example by living a godly life is powerful, and nurturing a lifestyle of study in a young person will give them a head start on the straight path. Critical thinking partnered with a love for God and His Word makes for a solid follower of Jesus.

I have hidden your word in my heart that
I might not sin against you.

PSALM 119:11 NIV

NO SUCH THING AS PERFECT

"Farewell to those who want an entirely pure and purified church. This is plainly wanting no church at all."

While the sacrifice of Jesus has justified us in the eyes of God, we are continually being sanctified and transformed into His likeness over the course of our lives. It is a process empowered by the Holy Spirit that requires our active participation.

James 4:8 says, *"Draw near to God and He will draw near to you. Cleanse your hands, you sinners; and purify your hearts, you double-minded."* Notice the emphasis on you and your. If each member of your congregation dedicated themselves to their own purification, then the whole of the church would be for the better. Extend the same grace and mercy God has shown you to your brothers and sisters. Though some may be farther along or just beginning their journey of being transformed, we are in this together.

"Then the master called the servant in . . . 'I canceled all that debt of yours because you begged me to. Shouldn't you have had mercy on your fellow servant just as I had on you?'"

MATTHEW 18:32-33 NIV

SING TO GOD!

"The devil should not be allowed to keep all the best tunes for himself."

The right song can transform a room. A catchy tune will play, and a crowd of people will begin bobbing their heads, tapping their fingers, swaying from side to side, or even joining the melody in song or dance. There is something about a good rhythm that evokes movement in people, across all the world's regions and cultures.

The desire to use the vocal chords, feet, and hands He gave us to express ourselves in this way is something that brings joy to God and this is evident in the way God is worshipped in Scripture. The Psalms speak of clapping, dancing, singing, shouting, and playing a variety of instruments—all in praise to God.

So if you find a new song on the tip of your tongue, however simple it is, sing it out to your Creator who delights in His creation.

"I will praise the name of God with a song, and will magnify him with thanksgiving."

PSALM 69:30

ACCEPT GOD'S CALL

"Be content in the calling God has placed you. I have not learned it yet."

When we consider the idea of calling, our imaginations often run to extremes such as third-world missions, influential career paths, positions in church government, or even political positions.

Consider the diverse group of people God used for His purposes in His Word. Most did not have grand beginnings or great positions of power, the foremost example of which is Jesus Himself. There was nothing glorious by human standards about His time on earth. He washed fishermen's feet, He taught the uneducated with parables, He ate with sinners—yet He was completely content and humble because He knew the glory that was ahead of Him. He was in tune with His Father and therefore confident and envisioned for present and future.

The ripple effects of a simple word or action are beyond our comprehension, therefore no calling is insignificant if God is involved. If you are unsure or feeling discouraged about your calling, get in tune with Your Father.

"But now hath God set the members every one of them in the body, as it hath pleased Him."

1 CORINTHIANS 12:18

MARITAL BLISS

"To have peace and love in a marriage is a gift that is next to the knowledge of the gospel."

Modern marriage has been sadly reduced to a state-recognized contract and a cocktail of short-lived thrills, resulting in high divorce rates and a decline in marriages in general.

For the Christian, marriage is more than a piece of paper or a whirlwind romance, but a covenantal reflection of Christ and His bride. With covenant in mind, every facet of the Christ-centered marriage reveals something beautiful about our relationship with God and every decision to extend grace and love to your spouse, even when it is difficult, becomes empowered by Him. United in vision, the love and peace a married couple can experience in their covenant is immeasurable.

Regardless of your marital status, the common denominator for happiness is a Christ-centered life.

"Two are better than one, because they
have a good return for their labor:
If either of them falls down, one can help
the other up…"

ECCLESIASTES 4:9-10 NIV

THE LAW NEEDS GRACE

"Without grace, the Law kills a man and increases sin."

Reflect for a moment on the old testament. God's holy standard was set in literal stone and His people were required to shed blood and obey an elaborate set of laws to atone for their sins. Even then, the story of the Israelites was rife with violence and unfaithfulness to God that led to much suffering. The perfect law only highlighted humanity's incapability to bridge the gap created by sin. Something more than the blood of animals was needed to cleanse and restore us to God's pure design.

With mercy and compassion, Jesus came to bridge that gap with the undeniable, irrevocable, and purifying power of His grace. It is His grace that fills all the gaps of our inadequacy to make us whole again in Him and enables us to confidently pursue holiness according to His law.

"But where sin abounded, grace did much more abound."

ROMANS 5:20

BEARING OTHERS' FAULTS

"The love towards our neighbors must be like the pure and chaste love between bride and bridegroom, where all faults are connived at [overlooked] and borne with, and only the virtues regarded."

A shift in customer service, an hour in rush hour traffic, or five minutes on the internet are enough to become frustrated with your fellow man. Rubbing shoulders with other human beings flawed in different ways than we are stirs up all kinds of emotions. In a moment, pride and ignorance can glaze over our awareness of our own sins with offense for the sins of another.

The parable of the unforgiving servant in Matthew 18 urges us to extend mercy and forgiveness, because of the great mercy we have been extended. However holy you are, your righteousness alone will never be enough for salvation. We are all justified and saved by

Jesus Christ alone. In humility, remember that we are all human beings in a tug-of-war between our flesh and our spirit, and show grace to your fellow man.

Above all, love each other deeply, because love covers over a multitude of sins.

1 PETER 4:8 NIV

AN ASTONISHING DEATH

"The greatest wonder ever on earth is, that the Son of God died the shameful death of the cross. It is astonishing, that the Father should say to his only Son, who by nature is God: Go, let them hang thee on gallows."

Take a moment and ponder the magnificence, the infinitude, and the power of God. He is our Creator. He has no origin, but is the origin Himself. He set time and space into motion, and he designed our ecosystems and our nervous systems down to the very cell. The power to be omniscient and omnipotent is unimaginable to the human mind.

And yet, He left His throne in heaven and came down to earth as a human baby. He worked as a carpenter, He kept the company of fishermen, tax collectors, and prostitutes. His teachings drew crowds whom He, in compassion for them, miraculously multiplied food to feed and care for. And lastly, the Son of the God of the universe suffered mockery, torture, and death at the hands of His creation. In the end, He rose to glory and now invites us to join Him in the inheritance of heaven. It truly is an astonishing gospel.

"Yet it was the Lord's will to crush him and cause him to suffer . . . For he bore the sin of many, and made intercession for transgression for the transgressors."

ISAIAH 53:10,12

KEEP THE WORD PURE

"No greater mischief can happen to a Christian people, than to have God's word taken from them, or falsified, so that they no longer have it pure and clear."

Martin Luther recognized false beliefs in his time that were instilled in the Church as Catholic doctrine not based in the Word of God. Common people who did not have the education or access to read the Bible themselves placed their trust in leaders who did. Unfortunately, greed was rampant in the Church in the form of indulgences—documents that claimed to minimize punishment in the afterlife that were purchased by the recipient for themselves or on the behalf of a loved one who already passed. This created the belief that salvation and the forgiveness of sins was achieved by works, not by faith in the finished work of Christ and true repentance.

We are fortunate to live in an age where the Bible is accessible and readable by most, but there is still no shortage of voices out there that attempt to manipulate it's words for their own gain. Wash yourself regularly in the pure Word of God and keep a clean mind.

Jesus answered,
"It is written: 'Man shall not live on bread alone, but on every word that comes from the mouth of God.'"

MATTHEW 4:4 NIV

TRUTH WITH ABILITY

*"All laws and philosophy merely tell us what should be done,
but they do not provide the strength to do it."*

We all know what it is like to know you ought to do something, but struggle to find the ability to convert that knowledge into action. If you were not so blessed to be a morning person, you are likely a seasoned veteran in the battle of alarms and sunrise. To my brothers and sisters fighting sleepy mornings, I remind you of the word of Jesus to His very own sleepy disciples: "The spirit is willing, but the flesh is weak."

Fortunately, if you are born again and filled with the Holy Spirit, you have immense power within you to overcome any obstacle. To quote Jesus again, "With man this is impossible, but with God all things are possible." So whether it's something as simple as getting out of bed in the morning or as complex as rocket science, tap into the power of God through faith for whatever obstacle you are facing this morning.

"For when we were yet without strength, in due time Christ died for the ungodly."

ROMANS 5:6

THE ONLY COMFORTER

"Without Christ no one can comfort himself."

To be human is to be finite and fragile. We feel this more than ever in the valleys of life that we all experience at some point like loss, suffering, and hardship. In these times we can feel powerless to help and unable to cope with circumstances beyond our control. We can find solidarity with people who understand what we are going through from mutual experience or empathy, but sometimes it feels like there is no true comfort to be found.

This is where you can run into the shelter of the able arms of God who does not share our fragility, but is infinitely strong, who knows your heart without a word, and gives supernatural peace. You can find comfort that you are never truly alone in this world, but are being watched over by a compassionate Father who is not unaffected by your pain. Cling to the Rock in the midst of the waves and He will calm your storms.

"Do not let your hearts be troubled.
You believe in God; believe also in me."

JOHN 14:1 NIV

THE SPIRIT AND
THE WORD AGREE

"Whenever a man reads the Word of God, the Holy Spirit is speaking to him."

J anuary arrived and, like many Christians at that time of year, Clarice began her annual Bible plan anew. She reveled in the wonder of the creation story, grieved the fall of Man, celebrated the faith of Abraham, and marveled at the works of God through Moses. Then came the tough meat. Leviticus. Numbers. But while she was struggling through, she came upon a verse in Numbers 23: *"God is not human, that he should lie, not a human being, that he should change his mind. Does he speak and then not act? Does he promise and not fulfill?"*

Recently, Clarice was feeling discouraged with her life. There was no sign of promises she felt God had made coming to pass anytime soon. The verse jumped off the page, as if it was written personally for her, even though she had read it many times. Immediately she felt seen by God, assured of His faithfulness, and left her daily Bible reading with renewed trust.

Don't neglect regular consumption of the Word of God. The Spirit has something special to share with you every time you sit down read.

For the word of God is alive and active. Sharper than any double-edged sword, it penetrates even to dividing soul and spirit, joints and marrow; it judges the thoughts and attitudes of the heart.

HEBREWS 4:12 NIV

SATAN A PREACHER?

"The devil, too, can quote Scripture. But his use of Scripture is defective. He does not quote it completely but only so much of it as serves his purpose. The rest he silently omits."

It is an unfortunate truth that much evil has been done in the name of God by deceived and self-seeking Christians throughout history. Slavery and racism were at one point justified by Christians cherry-picking and manipulating scripture. Authentic misogyny and abuse have been condoned by certain circles by taking the apostle Paul's words out of context. The catholic church once justified paid indulgences with scripture to fund their greed. Since it's been written, God's word has been misused by man for all sorts of sinful purposes. This is why prayerful and thorough study of the Bible is required so we don't misrepresent our Lord on Earth and contribute to our tainted reputation.

Make a pact with God today to never turn to His word with selfish ambition. Do not join Satan in his crafty misdirection and manipulation of the words of God—go to scripture with a humility and seek out the true heart of our Father.

Submit yourselves, then, to God.
Resist the devil, and he will flee from you.

JAMES 4:7 NIV

THE BUILDING OF GOD

"We do not know how our Lord God is preparing His structure. We see only the scaffolding of stakes and ropes . . . But in the future life we shall see the structure and building of God and, filled with wonder . . . we shall rejoice at having endured the trials."

Most Christians could probably attest to times they have wondered in confusion, and sometimes frustration, what God is up to. It can be easy to look at our lives, the lives of those around us, and even the world and think, *Surely God should do something about that. Why isn't He? Will He?*

I am certain that Noah had similar thoughts as he built the ark. And Moses, who led God's people through the wilderness, never to see or taste the fruit of the promised land himself. I can only imagine the moments of doubt creeping in for the disciples as Jesus's body was taken down from the cross.

The common denominator with these figures is that they continued on in the faith and trusted God. And we who can read the accounts of their lives thousands of years later know that their faith was no small contribution to the ultimate building of God's kingdom. Therefore, be encouraged in your own fight of faith today. God is faithful!

"Therefore, since we also have such a great cloud of witnesses surrounding us, let's rid ourselves of every obstacle and the sin which so easily entangles us, and let's run with endurance the race that is set before us . . ."

HEBREWS 12:1 NASB

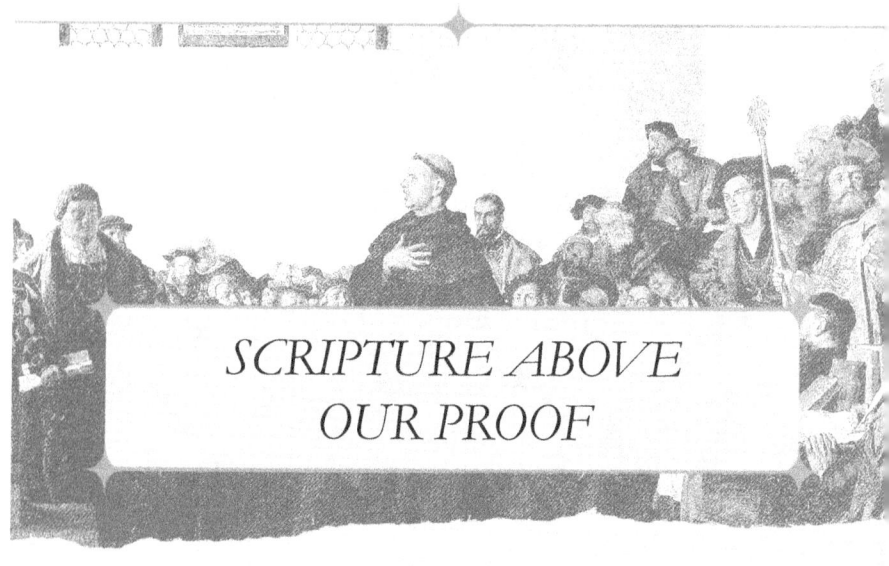

SCRIPTURE ABOVE OUR PROOF

"An orthodox person gives the glory to God and does not doubt that everything has been put down well and correctly in Scripture, even though he may not know how to prove everything."

A common point of contention with Christianity for unbelievers is the authenticity of the Bible. It's a question many Christians have also pondered at some point in their walk with God: how do I know the Bible is legitimate? How can a book with forty authors and innumerable translations over thousands of years be the true and unadulterated Word of God?

There are many schools of thought regarding the infallibility of scripture—some like Luther abide by *sola scriptura*, some believe parts to be metaphorical, some entirely denounce some statements as outdated and irrelevant. Such a foundational belief is one to be prayerfully and soberly studied out yourself. Ultimately, there are things we will never understand on this side of eternity and this is where faith comes in. Research, consult with a knowledgeable leader in your local church, and keep your heart open to the Holy Spirit in your quest for truth. His wisdom transcends human intellect.

For since the creation of the world God's invisible qualities—his eternal power and divine nature—have been clearly seen, being understood from what has been made, so that people are without excuse.

ROMANS 1:20 NIV

HUMAN NATURE

"Man is by nature unable to want God to be God. Indeed he himself wants to be God, and does not want God to be God."

A father glanced up from his laptop to see his four-year-old daughter staring longingly at a glass jar on the kitchen counter—half-full of cookies his wife baked the day before. It was 9am, too early for cookies. The understanding father smiled with amusement at the childish moral dilemma.

So focused on her prize, the little girl was completely unaware of her silent observer as she clumsily dragged over a small stepping stool and began to reach for the cookie jar. Stealthily lifting the lid, she grabbed a chocolate chip cookie from the pile and took a bite of it.

Her father called in slight surprise, "Sweetie, what are you doing?"

Startled, she dropped the cookie and hid her chocolate-smeared hands behind her back. "Nothing, daddy!"

The father's surprise grew. With lips covered in cookie crumbles, she had just lied to him. *Where did she learn to lie? I didn't teach her that.* After a moment, he scooped her up in his arms and spoke gently with a knowing smile, "How about we go play at the park until lunch, hm?"

Our selfish nature isn't taught, but we are born striving against it. We are all born in need of a supernatural Savior.

"As the heavens are higher than the earth,
so are my ways higher than your ways and
my thoughts than your thoughts."

ISAIAH 55:9 NIV

GOVERNMENT BEGINS IN THE HOME

"If obedience is not rendered in the homes, we shall never have a whole city, country, principality, or kingdom well-governed."

No amount of worldly legislation or policy can change the human heart. Atrocities such as murder, assault, drug dealing, and human trafficking continue to happen even though it is illegal. This is frequently reflected in the Bible, particularly in the Old Testament. The heart of man is corrupt. The law alone wasn't enough. Love had to come to fulfill it.

Jesus came and made the ultimate display of love: laying down His life and cleansing us with His blood to make a way for us to be born again as vessels for His glory. Now with Christ dwelling within us, our hearts can be transformed into His likeness and so can our homes. By the power of God, the roots of turmoil in our country such as fatherlessness, abuse, and addiction can be healed. Jesus alone is our hope and that hope grows when we outwork this transformation in our homes.

"If you love me, keep my commands."

JOHN 14:15 NIV

THE LEAST GIFT

"Wealth is the smallest thing on earth, the least gift that God has bestowed on mankind."

A rguably the greatest object of desire for humans worldwide is money. Crimes are committed, lives are ruined, environments are decimated all for the pursuit of wealth. Wealth also enables better healthcare, better education, and home-ownership. Money is required to live and operate in society, but most would be happy with just *a little bit more* than they actually need. Something so important to people must also be important to God, right? Yes, but not in the way you might think.

Jesus spoke at length about money, but it wasn't His top 10 tips to get your first $100,000 or what stock to invest into. The kingdom of God is an inside-out kingdom—the humble are exalted and the exalted are humbled. Note the spiritual gifts mentioned in 1 Corinthians 12 and how wealth and status are not among them. We've already won heaven's jackpot with salvation through Jesus, but God's concern is with the motives of the heart and the pursuit of godliness.

"Do not store up for yourselves treasures on earth, where moths and vermin destroy, and where thieves break in and steal. But store up for yourselves treasures in heaven . . . For where your treasure is, there your heart will be also."

MATTHEW 6:19-21 NIV

THE PURPOSE OF
MINISTRY

*"It is the work and the glory of the ministry to make real
saints out of sinners, living souls out of the dead, saved souls
out of the damned, children of God out of servants of the
devil."*

C hris was the worship leader in the heart of
his city. He had a radical conversion story that
gripped the hearts of many in his area, which
quickly grew into a thriving youth outreach and then into
worship leadership. His passion for praise and intimate
connection to God spilled over into the room in a tangible
way, drawing crowds and increasing the congregation.

But somewhere in the glow of stage lights, Chris's
focus shifted from authentic worship to impressing with
performance and appearance. Pride muddied the waters
and the air that was once electric with the presence of
God began to feel stale.

It wasn't until Chris saw a familiar face in the crowd

that he was shaken out of his spiritual coma. It was an old friend from his youth. They parted ways when Chris accepted Christ and left the party scene, with his friend falling deeper into drugs. He reconnected with him immediately after the service and a lightning bolt of revelation struck Chris: he had become distracted and forgotten the love that found him at his darkest point. At that moment, his vision was renewed. God's heart is to find those who were lost, just as we all were at one point.

And we all, who with unveiled faces contemplate the Lord's glory, are being transformed into his image with ever-increasing glory, which comes from the Lord, who is the Spirit.

2 CORINTHIANS 3:18 NIV

LESSONS OF LOVE

"Love teaches very readily how to conduct yourself well in all situations; and without it nothing whatever can be satisfactorily taught."

Two friends agreed to volunteer at their local soup kitchen to serve a thanksgiving meal to the needy in their city. One of them drives to the grocery story to pick up a few ingredients he signed up to bring. On the way, a mini-van cuts him off, causing him to brake hard. He growls and whips into the other lane, making frustrated gestures at the driver as he passes them. He scrambles through the crowded store to find his ingredients, paces in the long lines, and finally arrives at his destination.

The other friend was running late, stopped at a red-light. He had already been to busy grocery store, but instead of seeing the shoppers as obstacles from his destination, he smiled imagining all their families enjoying thanksgiving together later that day. With his armful of items, he allowed an old woman with a single bag of sugar to go ahead of him in line. He arrived at the soup kitchen with a bagful of blessings and a heart overflowing with love to give to those in need.

Both of these friends accomplished a good thing by offering their time to serve. But in their conduct we see the difference between "doing" and "being" love. When you become love, you don't have to strive to do kind or loving things—it comes from the overflow of your heart.

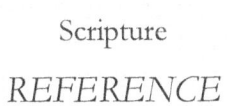

Scripture

REFERENCE

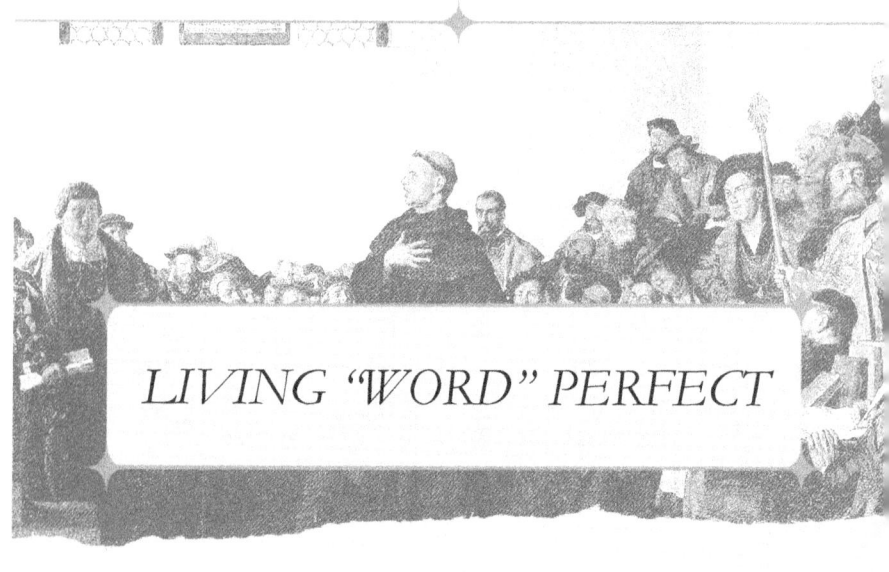

LIVING "WORD" PERFECT

"We should not consider the slightest error against the Word of God unimportant."

There is no doubt that a common error among Christians is taking scripture out of context. Only God knows how many misinterpretations have formed mindsets, theologies, or entire denominations that miss the mark on God's intention. The desire of the humble Christian is ultimately to set aside pride and agenda to glean the truth of God in His Word.

Some scriptures taken out of context can have incredibly harmful and deceitful effects. In our modern age, misguided and false teaching can spread like wildfire. This is why it is more important than ever to be a dedicated student of God's Word. To recognize a deception, you must have a firm grasp on the truth and a tender ear to the Holy Spirit to correct and combat it. Dedicate yourself anew today to keeping a solid footing in truth and a watchful eye for potential road hazards in your walk with God.

But there were false prophets also among the people, even as there shall be false teachers among you, who privily shall bring in damnable heresies, even denying the Lord that bought them, and bring upon themselves swift destruction.

2 PETER 2:1

THE WORLD'S EMPTY PROMISES

"The world promises great things but delivers few. It acts like hosts who give their guests too little and console them with empty words."

Wealth, power, fame—these are some of the most sought-after things in life. Those of us who don't have them believe our life would be better if we had them. But when you look closely at the lives of those who attain these desires, you more often than not find a life unfulfilled and longing for more. Many of these same people we think have it all end up with broken marriages, in scandals that cost them their freedom, or even addictions at the expense of their lives.

God can bless His children with wealth and success, but these things are only a byproduct of a fulfilling relationship with Him. He is our reward that transcends our time on this earth.

Command those who are rich in this
present world not to be arrogant nor to
put their hope in wealth, which is so
uncertain, but to put their hope in God,
who richly provides us with everything for
our enjoyment.

1 TIMOTHY 6:17 NIV

DID YOU KNOW

Luther's father sent him to university to become a
lawyer. Luther went through schooling in liberal arts,
receiving his Master's degree in 1505. Shortly after
enrolling in law, he pivoted to philosophy which he
ultimately found unsatisfying. His disillusionment
with human reasoning drove him deeper into
scripture.

THE DIVINE ABOVE
THE HUMAN

"The truth is mightier than eloquence, the Spirit greater than genius, faith more than education."

L uther learned this well in his early education in the liberal arts and philosophy. Ultimately, he found human reasoning apart from scripture unable to lead people to God. While intelligence and sophistication are things that people use to elevate themselves among each other in the world, one look at the people God used in the Bible breaks down our human idea of qualification.

David was a shepherd boy whose zeal for God makes him famous through his acts and psalms as "a man after God's own heart". While he came from humble beginnings and made many mistakes, it was for his dedication and repentant attitude that God showered his favor on him in the form of authority and blessing.

Paul was an educated and learned man, but relentlessly persecuted the young Church until he was humbled to blindness by the sight of Jesus on the road to Damascus. Only then by acknowledging and submitting to Jesus as Lord was he transformed from a tool of destruction to a builder of the early Church and largest contributor to the Bible.

Take these accounts of biblical icons as a personal encouragement against disqualifying yourself or others based on human judgment.

For it is written, I will destroy the wisdom
of the wise, and will bring to nothing the
understanding of the prudent.

1 CORINTHIANS 1:19

UNSEALING THE LETTER

"The New Testament is nothing but a revelation of the Old Testament, as if one were in possession of a sealed letter and then later on opened it."

Taken at face value, the Old Testament can seem like a strange mix of history, law, poetry, and prophecy. The mighty acts of God written across the text can make you wonder—*where are His mighty acts today?* The detailed instruction and law scribed by Moses, the emphasis on sacrifice, and Israel's tug-of-war with God . . . what does it all mean and how is it relevant to me today?

Then in comes Jesus. He fulfills the law and the prophecies, making Himself the ultimate sacrifice that the blood of a million lambs could not accomplish. And He gives us the Holy Spirit, arming us with same power that raised Him from the dead to do mighty acts in His name.

Commit yourself to studying out these truths and parallels with a sensitive ear to the Spirit and watch the words jump out from the page. They are precious gems that require some digging to uncover.

The law is only a shadow of the good things that are coming—not the realities themselves. For this reason it can never, by the same sacrifices repeated endlessly year after year, make perfect those who draw near to worship.

HEBREWS 10:1 NIV

FLYING FRIED CHICKEN

"He doesn't not want me to sit at home, to loaf, to commit matters to God, and to wait till fried chicken flies into my mouth. That would be tempting God."

Most Christians have experienced a season of life where you are waiting on God—whether that be for help making a life decision, in a crisis of faith, or waiting for supernatural provision. But waiting does not mean simply letting time pass. God is not glorified by us twiddling our thumbs in hopes that He'll show up.

The writer of Ecclesiastes advises: *"Sow your seed in the morning, and at evening let your hands not be idle, for you do not know which will succeed, whether this or that, or whether both will do equally well."* (Ecclesiastes 11:6) We're called to be an active people, even in our waiting. If you're waiting on God for financial provision, continue to seek out opportunity and don't neglect your work. If you're a couple considering having children, pray and study together about godly parenthood. In your waiting, be actively seeking, and God will be faithful to answer.

Therefore my beloved brethren, be ye steadfast, unlovable, always abounding in the work of the Lord.

1 CORINTHIANS 15:58

HIGH-SPIRITED MINISTERS

"He must be of a high and great spirit that undertakes to serve the people in body and soul, for he must suffer the utmost danger and unthankfulness."

L eadership is not just a buzzword nor a rank to idolize or envy. Ask a student in bible college what they want to do after they graduate and half of them will say they want to become a youth pastor or a missionary. It is an admirable desire, but being a leader is no easy task. Those are take on the mantle of leadership are charged with a high bar of conduct and responsibility for those they oversee. Their role of service and guidance can put a target on their back for spiritual attack. It's an often thankless, unglamorous job that can only be accomplished by a man or woman dependent on God for strength.

Pray for the leaders in your life, thank them for all that they do, and go out of your way to bless them in some way!

Since an overseer manages God's household . . . he must be hospitable, one who loves what is good, who is self-controlled, upright, holy and disciplined. He must hold firmly to the trustworthy message as it has been taught, so that he can encourage others by sound doctrine and refute those who oppose it.

TITUS 1:7-9 NIV

DID YOU KNOW

After being ordered to appear before an assembly of the Holy Roman Empire in Worms, including the Emperor Charles V himself, Luther was presented with a collection of his writings they wished him to recant. He refused, and not much later an edict was made that declared him an outlaw, banned his works, called for his arrest, and even permitted his death without legal consequence.

A LOVE-HATE RELATIONSHIP

"God loves and hates temptations. He loves them when they provoke us to pray to Him and trust in Him; He hates them when we despair because of them."

W hen the word "temptation" is spoken in the presence of Christians, often the first feelings that arise are those of guilt and shame. We feel ashamed of the residue of sinful desire even though we have known the light of the salvation of God in our lives. The whispers of the enemy can quickly bog down the mind of the Christian: *If you really loved God, you wouldn't want that. If you were really saved, you wouldn't think that way. You are the same sinner you've always been and you always will be.*

Jesus famously combated similar challenges when he was tempted in the wilderness after His baptism. Even being tempted in the way He was, He did not sin, but prevailed and left the wilderness empowered to begin His ministry.

Temptation itself isn't sin. Don't let your humanity cause you to shrink inwards in despair, but draw closer to God who delights to help you and transform you into who He designed you to be.

The testing of your faith develops perseverance. Perseverance must finish its work so that you may be mature and complete, not lacking anything.

JAMES 1:3-4 NIV

REASON FALLS SHORT

"Reason is . . . a beautiful light. But it cannot [alone] . . . find the path that will lead from sin and from death to righteousness and to life; it remains in darkness."

The intellect and mind of man is an amazing thing. Even in the last fifty years, we have made leaps in technological innovation, medical advancements, and beautiful artwork in many forms. Apart from God however, this intelligence meant to cause the Earth to thrive can be twisted into self-worship and greed at the expense of fellow man and the state of the planet. With all these advancements, philosophers bitterly debate the origin and meaning of life with many reaching the conclusion that there is no purpose at all. We make ourselves gods and what pathetic gods we make.

Without the light of God, we can go down a dark

MARTIN LUTHER'S *Little Instruction Book*

path with our own reasoning. Where human wisdom tapers off, God is there with vast knowledge beyond comprehension and with kindness to reveal wonders in the secret place. Take a drink of the living water and have your deep needs met by the guiding light of God.

But of him are ye in Christ Jesus, who of God is made unto us wisdom, and righteousness, and sanctification, and redemption.

1 CORINTHIANS 1:30

LOVE LOOKS LIKE GOD

"*The more a person loves, the closer he approaches the image of God.*"

Love is a powerful feeling. It is the subject of numerous songs and poems, the daydream of the young, and the cherished memory of the old. Human love is often tainted with selfish ambition and lust, but arguably one of the purest forms of love possible for a human to experience is that of a parent.

After months of anticipation and preparation, that warm little bundle is placed in your arms and immediately you know you would do anything and everything for this baby. You'll wipe away their tears, put bandaids on skinned knees, rejoice when they rejoice, and hold them close as long as they let you. It feels as if nothing they ever do could change how much you love them.

This is merely a glimpse and a shadow of what our heavenly Father feels for us and the lengths He is willing to go for us. Whether you are fortunate to be a parent or not, where there is love between the people of God, we glow with His presence.

Dear friends, let us love one another, for love comes from God. Everyone who loves has been born of God and knows God. Whoever does not love does not know God, because God is love.

1 JOHN 4:7-8 NIV

HOPE FOR THE BEST

*"In all matters we should hope and pray for the best;
nevertheless, we should be prepared for the worst."*

ope and faith are often what we cling to in
times of trouble and intermingle to sustain us. In times of difficulty or anticipat-
ing change, sometimes we blind ourselves to any other
possible outcome other than the one we are pressing
in for in an attempt at bolstering our faith. And when
things don't turn out like we planned, we are left ill-
equipped for the result and occasionally our faith
rocked, asking, *Why didn't God come through for me?*

The oft-spoken phrase, "God works in mysterious
ways", though not in the Bible, captures some truth
that is better expressed in Isaiah 55:8, *"For my thoughts
are not your thoughts, neither are your ways my ways."*

Placing all our bets on a particular scenario of resolution limits the much better options God could have in store. Don't mistake stubbornness or close-mindedness for faith. Have hope, but ultimately let it be a hope submitted to God and you cannot go wrong.

Hope deferred makes the heart sick, but a longing fulfilled is a tree of life.

PROVERBS 13:12 NIV

A CHEERFUL CREATION

"God wants us to be cheerful, and He hates sadness. For had He wanted us to be sad, He wouldn't have given us the sun, the moon, and the various fruits of the earth. All these He gave for our good cheer."

T hink back to Genesis: the vast array of creatures, the rolling landscape, the abundance of fruit, the lush garden. God breathed life into dust and man was created to keep peaceful domain over what He made. God said it was good. How could anyone be sad in this haven He created? Sorrow entered the world when sin entered the world.

Sorrow is an emotion we all experience in varying degrees at some point in our lives. Grief, depression, loneliness, and heartbreak are all negative feelings that can overshadow the beauty in life.

If you find yourself low on cheer, spend some time

in creation. Though this earth is tainted by sin, the birds sing, the butterflies flutter, and the leaves in the trees sway gracefully in the wind just as they would have in Eden. Revelation talks of the new heaven and new earth, where there is no death and no tears. Until Jesus returns to restore all the earth, take heart in the purity of what He joyfully created.

"Sing O heavens; and be joyful, O earth;
and break forth into singing,
O mountains: for the Lord hath
comforted his people, and will have mercy
upon his afflicted."

ISAIAH 49:13

THE PERFECT
WEDDING RING

*"Faith is the wedding ring with which we have pledged
ourselves to Christ."*

The modern purpose of marriage is primarily companionship and stability. Many share the sentiment that marriage is simply a piece of paper recognized by the government, a spark that inevitably dies out, and the divorce rates reflect this. What was intended to be leadership has become control, intimacy has become lust, and love has become a currency.

What has been lost is the meaningful design that God has woven into marriage. Not only were men and women joined together in marriage for companionship, partnership, and procreation, but as a symbol of something much bigger: Jesus's unconditional love and his imminent return. Paul makes this connection in Ephesians 5, instructing husbands to love their wives as Christ loves the church and for wives to submit to their husbands as the church submits to Christ. When we grasp this beautiful truth, that married life is a reflection of Jesus's love for us—new depths of love and are unlocked. Whether you are married or not, the symbol of this miraculous union is still relevant. Let your faith be a vow to the Bridegroom.

. . .as a bridegroom rejoices over his bride,
so will your God rejoice over you.

ISAIAH 62:5 NIV

CENTRAL DOCTRINE

"Now the article of justification, which is our sole defense, not only against all the force and craft of man, but also against the gates of hell, is this: that by faith only in Christ, and without works, we are pronounced righteous and saved."

Accomplishment, education, and recognition holds an incredibly high value in a world where our resumes often determine our worth and enable (or deny) entrance into higher levels of society. Relationships suffer and fail over contribution or performance deemed inadequate by each other. Everywhere human beings create standards and everywhere human beings fall short of them. So it is that we've been trained since youth that what you do, how much you do, and how well you do it decides your value.

These worldly ideals are turned upside down by the word of God. Status on earth is nontransferable—it is the work of Christ alone that justifies us in the eyes of God. It is when the Christian can come to this place of humility and acknowledgment of God, that our work on Earth becomes truly effective.

Let these truths create a kind and merciful heart in you towards your fellow man, and grace for yourself as well.

For by grace are ye saved through faith; and that not of yourselves: it is the gift of God: Not of works, lest any man should boast.

EPHESIANS 2:8-9

MASQUERADING AS VIRUE

"These two sins, hatred and pride, deck and trim themselves out, as the devil clothed himself, in the Godhead. Hatred will be godlike; pride will be truth."

We need not look further for an example of these things than the relationship between Jesus and his greatest critics: the pharisees and sadducees.

The gospels begin a time where Israel is under the oppressive rule of the Romans. Many prayed for the coming of a Messiah that would overthrow this government with might and glory. But when the humble son of a carpenter begins teaching divine wisdom locally, with miracles and crowds in tow, they are taken aback. Jesus could see right through their farce of righteousness and virtue and called them out as "whitewashed tombs". With the pride of the pharisees wounded by his words of conviction, their self-seeking is re-vealed in anger and soon they are plotting his death. They condemned Him to a common criminal's death, but ultimately we know He rose again in conquest over death.

Consider the dichotomy of the mask of godliness worn by the pharisees who prayed and fasted for all to see, and the humility of Christ who came to serve and save. Strive for authenticity with a humble heart and let your boasting be in the merciful love of God.

. . . because human anger does not produce the righteousness that God desires.

JAMES 1:20

PRATTLE AND PREACH

"Since we are preaching to children, we must also prattle with them."

nyone who has ever taught children knows the truth of Luther's statement here. Children typically have lower attention spans and struggle to sit still or be quiet for long and this is not a character fault, it is simply stage of development. They are bursting with life and energy—is it more important to force them to sit quietly in a seat for hours on end or to instill a life-long thirst for knowledge and learning?

Most adults, in all our sophistication, have lost the joy and vibrancy of childhood. Some had their spirits broken and dreams squashed by adults who prioritized their own peace and convenience over their development. For these reasons it may feel unnatural to "prattle" to a child as you teach them. Remember Jesus's treatment of children—when His disciples scolded them, He drew them near with joy and spoke highly of their perceived lowly status. Let the kind and humble heart of Jesus shine through you in your engagement with children.

Jesus said, "Let the little children come to me, and do not hinder them, for the kingdom of heaven belongs to such as these."

MATTHEW 19:14 NIV

STOP AND WEAR OUT

"If I rest, I rust."

Every human being on earth needs rest. We are finite beings that are subject to mental and physical fatigue. Physical fatigue can usually be righted with a good night's sleep. Mental and emotional fatigue is more complicated and often requires techniques unique to each person. The problem at hand is *resting well.*

Is Luther is denouncing rest as a whole? No, rather rest that results in stagnancy, idleness, and laziness. Healthy rest is rest that truly replenishes you and invigorates you towards your goals and duties. Similar to the concept of waiting on God, rest is not sitting on your hands and letting time go by. Authentic rest varies from person to person, but ultimately God is the one who meets our deep needs, sustains us, and gives us what we need to conquer the day.

A little sleep, a little slumber, a little folding of the hands to rest—and poverty will come on you like a thief and scarcity like an armed man.

PROVERBS 6:10-11 NIV

HUMILITY'S GREATEST EXAMPLE

"'Tis a high example, that he so deeply humbled himself and suffered, who created the whole world, heaven and earth."

P ride is sneaky. In a world where being self-made is one of the highest strengths, pride thrives in independence and achievement. If you ever catch yourself feeling offended, judging your fellow man, or revolving your life around the impressions of others, return to the gospels.

There is no one who has been more entitled to praise, no one whose significance could be more understated than Jesus Christ. He is cosmic royalty, the son of God, creator of the universe. Accompanied by a legion of trumpeting angels, He could have descended from the heavens on a cloud of glory and power and demanded our worship. In the gospels, we see Satan egging Jesus on to do just that. Instead he was born in a barn, coming into the world covered in amniotic fluid as each and every one of us did. He leveled with humanity by teaching in parables, he made himself a servant by washing feet, and made himself a sacrifice by dying on a cross. If Jesus lived among us with compassion, patience, purity, and complete humility, what right do we have as Christian to conduct ourselves in any other way?

"Who being in the form of God . . . took upon him the form of a servant, and was made in the likeness of men, . . . he humbled himself and became obedient unto death, even the death of the cross."

PHILIPPIANS 2:6-8

SECOND ONLY TO THE HOLY GHOST

"In domestic affairs I defer to [my wife] Katie. Otherwise, I am led by the Holy Ghost."

"He who finds a wife, finds a good thing," says the Proverbs. There is a misconception among Christians who hold traditional family values that male headship means female inferiority and subservience, when that couldn't be further from the truth. God saw His creation Adam and knew he needed a partner. He created Eve from Adam's own flesh as a helper and companion to be trusted. His design for marriage was not for men to exercise control over their spouses, but to be humble enough to accept the help women were created to give.

Proverbs 31 describes the wife of noble character, who works diligently and with strength in and out of the home, speaks with wisdom, and conducts herself with honor and compassion. The godly man doesn't see a strong woman as a threat, but enables her to be the helper God made her to be.

If you are lucky enough to be a man married to a godly woman, acknowledge and thank her for her role in your life.

Who can find a virtuous woman? For her price is far above rubies. The heart of her husband doth safely trust in her, so that he shall have no need of spoil.

PROVERBS 31:10-11

THE PLAGUE
OF IDLENESS

*"For to be full and idle is the greatest plague on earth;
it is the trouble whence all other plagues come."*

I f you've ever read through Proverbs, you
know of the "character" referred to as the
sluggard. The sluggard is lazy, indulgent, and
neglectful to his own ruin. He contrasts the example
of the wise man, who is promised reward and honor
for his diligence, discipline, and humility.

We see similar example of this in the gospels with
the parable of the talents. Each servant was given a
different amount of money and each was judged by
what they did with what they were given. One servant
simply buried what he had, while the others used their
money to make more. The lesson we learn here spoken
by the master is if you are faithful with what you have

been given, more will be added to you. There is no set pace of hustle and grind, but to simply steward the gift of life well.

Don't bury the gift of God with idleness. God has placed something in the hands of everyone, according to their ability, and all you have to do is care for it and grow it with diligence.

By much slothfulness the building decayeth; and through idleness of the hands the house droppeth through.

ECCLESIASTES 10:18

MUSIC–GOD'S GIFT

"I have no use for cranks who despise music, because it is a gift of God. Next after theology, I give to music the highest place and the greatest honor."

David, one of the great men of our faith, was clearly a fan of music. The book of Psalms is full of exhortations of praise in the form of singing, clapping, and making music with a variety of instruments. When Saul was being tormented by an evil spirit in 1 Samuel 16, David was called in to play his lyre, and the evil spirit would leave him.

Music has a wonderful way of unlocking the inner dwellings of the human heart, and bringing joy and comfort. While mind, body, and spirit can operate and feel so separate, the making of music brings all these things together into an outward flow of sound. Surely the Designer of the skillful hands, creativity, and focused minds appreciates these things all coming together in praise to Him!

Come, let us sing for joy to the Lord;
let us shout aloud to the Rock of our
salvation. Let us come before him with
thanksgiving and extol him with music
and song.

PSALM 95:1-2 NIV

DID YOU KNOW

Luther was a prolific writer of music, having written
36 hymns in his native tongue of German designed
to be sung in church, school, home, or in public. He
wrote music to help people from all classes and ages
understand the gospel and memorize scripture.

A PRICKLY SITUATION

"We want to avoid the punishment of sin; we even want to resist it and defend our sin. We shall succeed as well as the dog that bites into the spines of a porcupine."

E very parent knows this equation: children + sugar = chaos. No matter how many times an adult warns them about potential tummy aches, children are often blissfully ignorant to the consequences—the immediate reward of saccharine sweetness of candy on the tastebuds is all they care about. The sugar high bursts in an explosion of energy and a mess of plastic wrappers, but just as quickly the crash leads to the prophesied tummy aches and grumpy attitudes.

A diet with consistent excess sugar leads to a variety of health problems, and in the same way, habitual sin can be the gravest of all. When you're sating your appetite with cheap imitations, the hunger for authentic fulfillment that comes with obedience and relationship with God is dulled.

With maturity comes consciousness of health, and you realize that your parents didn't spend all those nights reminding you to eat your broccoli for kicks. Stop settling for less: listen to the voice of your heavenly Father and come to the table of spiritual nourishment and growth He's laid out for you.

For the wages of sin is death . . .

ROMANS 6:22

AN EMPIRE FOR A ROSE

"If a man could make a single rose, an empire should be given him. But, because of their commonness, innumerable gifts of God are not appreciated."

E den was a midwest American teen, on the final stretch of high school and the cusp of adulthood. When an opportunity arose to join a mission trip to Africa, her burning desire to burst out of her local bubble drove her to sign up.

The culture shock was brutal. Unreliable power grids made air-conditioning a fever dream in the heat. Unpaved roads, unregulated traffic, and corrupt military checkpoints doubled the estimated duration of travel from one place to another. Unclean water sources, poor healthcare, under-equipped schools, and a history of civil war all made life difficult. And yet, life was abundant. Eden was met with smiling, curious children that were eager to learn. The markets were filled with vibrant patterns crafted by skilled fingers. Her group repaired a well that had been broken for a year, restoring clean drinking water to a village. She returned from her trip with a new perspective—one of gratitude and awareness of what she previously took for granted.

How true this sentiment rings not only for luxuries we enjoy in first-world countries, but the simple graces of God that sustain us day by day. Take a moment to identify some of these covert gifts and thank Him!

Enter his gates with thanksgiving and his courts with praise; give thanks to him and praise his name.

PSALM 100:4 NIV

WHAT CAN WE GIVE GOD?

"We cannot give God anything; for everything is already His, and all we have comes from Him. We can only give Him praise, thanks and honor."

Unless you have a special knack for gift-giving, most people know the struggle of selecting a gift for your father. He's an adult—if there is something he wants, he can usually just buy it himself. Perhaps you've already exhausted the options of tool sets, witty coffee mugs, and engraved pocket knives, or maybe your dad's interests don't align with the stereotypical "dad gifts". The older you get, the less material things matter. This is why more often than not, a heartfelt, handwritten card can mean so much more than an expensive gift. Words of love, specially knit together from the heart of their child, is enough to melt any father's heart.

It is even more so with our heavenly Father. What can we give Him that He doesn't already have? It is our whole-hearted devotion, our personal praise, and dedicated attention that He so desires.

"You are worthy, our Lord and God, to receive glory and honor and power, for you created all things, and by your will they were created and have their being."

REVELATION 4:11 NIV

HOW TO RECEIVE GRACE

"Certain it is that man must completely despair of himself in order to become fit to receive the grace of Christ."

A young boy was knelt in the middle of the living room floor, surrounded by scraps of wrapping paper and boxes. He tore open his new Lego set: an intricately-detailed spaceship, complete with a pilot and plastic laser beams.

His father looked on from the couch, already on his second cup of coffee since being awoken at the crack of dawn by his children. He smiled as his son puzzled at the amount of tiny pieces. He bought this set from his Christmas list, knowing it would challenge his ability, but indulging his independent streak.

An hour later, the son reached the end of the instruction book, but what he held in his hand did not match the picture on the box. Several times, he pulled it apart and attempted to replace pieces he had missed, but to no avail. He looked up at his father, attempting to blink away tears of frustration, and asked, "Dad, can you help me?"

"Of course, son," the father spoke graciously, "Let's start from the beginning."

How many times have we fooled ourselves into believing we know what we are doing and ended up with a less than satisfactory outcome? Tap into the grace of God—He's there to show you the way.

"Very truly I tell you, the Son can do nothing by himself; he can do only what he sees his Father doing, because whatever the Father does the Son also does."

JOHN 5:19 NIV

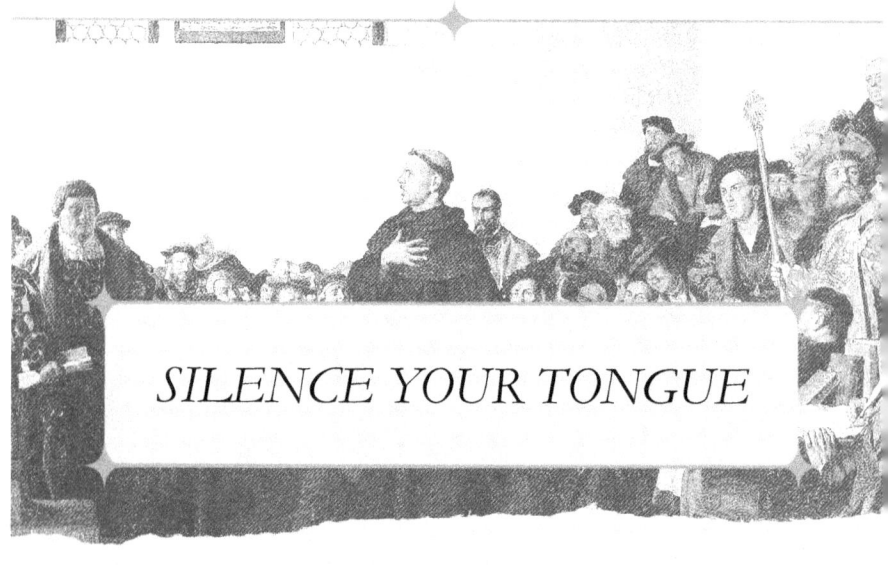

SILENCE YOUR TONGUE

"Men should think it over well and not obey anger which is hasty and has the word on the tongue and not in the heart."

The book of James describes the human tongue as untamable and likens it to the spark that sets a forest into flames. In the heat of an argument, even the most level-headed can become caught up in reactionary responses and end up saying something they regret.

Fortunately, God is slow to anger and abounding in love, and His Holy Spirit aids us in transforming into His likeness. We are made in His image after all!

Next time a harsh word is tickling the tip of your tongue, take a breath or even step away and let Jesus calm the storm brewing inside. Seek God's wisdom and let your words breathe life to those around you.

The tongue has the power of life and death, and those who love it will eat its fruit.

PROVERBS 18:21 NIV

DID YOU KNOW

Luther began teaching theology at the University of Wittenberg in 1508, where he received multiple degrees including a doctorate. In 1515, he was appointed as a vicar over two regions in Germany. It was over these years of studying and lecturing that he came to believe certain doctrine in the Catholic Church to be corrupt and missing essential truths of Christianity, sparking beginnings of the Reformation.

ENDING WELL

"God orders us to work and to do whatever our calling requires. Therefore he who looks to his calling and continues to work diligently, even if good fortune is against him and success fails to come for a while, is bound to fare well in the end."

It's very hard to maintain vision and hope for something you've devoted yourself to, without any fulfillment in sight. Perhaps you have consistently excelled at work with hopes of promotion, but haven't been recognized by your boss. Maybe you have a long-time friend you've had countless talks with about God, but they haven't come to Christ.

More and more, our culture has grown towards immediate gratification. Drive-thru's, streaming services, and two-day shipping have shortened our capacity for patience. Many verses speak of God blessing the righteous in this life, but everything points to living and working for ultimately eternal reward, the inheritance of every child of God.

Don't grow weary in your work—trust that at the end of the day God will provide exactly what you need. He is faithful.

And let us not be weary in well doing: for in due season we shall reap, if we faint not.

GALATIANS 6:9

THE CARPENTER
AND HIS WOOD

"He is the Carpenter, and we are the wood. His handiwork is the dear, the holy cross, which is bound to follow upon the teaching of the Gospel. He plies His tools and works on us, planes and carves us, in order to kill the old man within us."

Have you ever left an experience feeling like a different person? It might not necessarily have been a good experience—maybe you had a health scare, you were hurt by someone, or lost a loved one, the pain of which is a landmark in your life. Or perhaps something wonderful happened like meeting your spouse, landing a great job, or hitting a weight-loss goal.

All these things shape us in some way and can shift the trajectory of our lives. However, there is ultimately a great Designer at work who has wonderful plans for your life. In His wisdom, He can make something beautiful with the work of our lives. He wishes to sketch out a capable frame, carve a fluid shape of humility, and layer in colors of love, strength, and mercy. All you have to do is trust Him and allow Him to work.

But now, O Lord, thou art our father; we are the clay, and thou our potter; and we all are the work of thy hand.

ISAIAH 64:8

LIKE FATHER, LIKE SON

"Proud jackasses develop out of the sons of heroes who boast of the virtue of their fathers but make no effort to imitate it, dreaming instead that they, too, are heroes because they were born of heroes."

In the book of 1 Samuel, we are introduced to the childless wife Hannah who prays to God for a son. God heard her, and Samuel was born and dedicated to God. He was given to Eli, the priest and judge of Israel at the time, to raise in the house of God.

Eli was a godly man faithful to his duties, but his sons were wicked, stealing from sacrifices and sleeping with the women that worked at the entrance of the temple of meeting. They took for granted their stations as members of a family of priests, and dishonored the Lord. Even though Eli was overall a good man, he chose his sons over God by not dealing with their sin accordingly, and ultimately his whole family line was subject to the judgement of God because of their actions.

There is blessing from God in coming from a righteous family, but unless you reproduce that righteousness in your own life, the fruit of a family tree will be short-lived.

Listen, my sons, to a father's instruction;
pay attention and gain understanding. I
give you sound learning, so do not forsake
my teaching.

PROVERBS 4:1-2 NIV

RESTLESS PURSUITS

"The flesh is forever moving from present possessions to future ones. It loses the former in the pursuit of the latter and thus deprives itself of the use of both."

"**S**top and smell the roses" is a phrase you probably recognize. It can be hard to slow down and enjoy the present when there is so much to look forward to in the future. Perhaps you have a big goal you're working towards—maybe you're a parent working extra hours to save for your children's college or a newlywed in a small apartment with dreams of a house. Or maybe the present is difficult or painful, and you're hoping and praying for break-through on the horizon.

There are many reasons we can justify being hurriers and worriers, but Jesus Himself exhorts us in Matthew 6: "*. . . do not worry about tomorrow, for tomorrow will*

worry about itself. Each day has enough trouble of its own."
There's wisdom in being prepared, but not if it sacrifices enjoying the present. Take a day off and spend it with your kids. Be content with what you have until you can afford to upgrade. Acknowledge the pain of the present moment so you can savor the sweetness of joy to come. Take it one step at a time, and trust that the Lord will show you the way.

Do not boast about tomorrow, for you do not know what a day may bring.

PROVERBS 27:1 NIV

A HUNDRED THOUSAND
EXCUSES

"When I would speak and pray to God by myself, a hundred thousand hindrances at once intervene before I get at it. Then the devil can throw all sorts of reasons for delay into path."

A new year rings in and a circle of friends are sharing their new year's resolutions. One says, "I want to read a book every week." Another, "I'd like to lose 20 pounds this year." Mike spoke up, "I want to spend thirty minutes with God every morning."

The next morning, Mike woke up tired, but motivated. For the next month, he kept up his schedule. Then one morning he woke up particularly tired after a late night, and in his grogginess, he chose to skip his prayer time for today to get some extra sleep. On a Saturday, he took one look at his errands for the day and decided he didn't have time to pray. Another morning, he scrolled too long on his phone and was nearly late for work, with no time for prayer in the rush. With one distraction and seemingly justified reason after another, eventually the new habit was derailed.

Sometimes distractions are devices of the enemy, and sometimes it's simply the tug of our own desires that needs to be overcome. There are always going to be reasons to put off prayer, but none are truly more important than the need for communion with God.

Be sober, be vigilant; because your adversary the devil, as a roaring lion, walketh about, seeking whom he may devour.

1 PETER 4:8

HIS LIGHT BURDEN

There is no work on earth easier than the true service of God;
he loads us with no heavy burdens, but only asks that we
believe in him and preach of him.

G o to church every Sunday, spend time in
the Word every morning, raise your kids
to be godly adults, volunteer to help those
in need, evangelize your city, be an excellent worker,
maintain a godly marriage, love your neighbor, steward
your finances well—these are all commendable actions
that can feel a bit overwhelming when listed all at once.
Converting a godly, fruitful life into a checklist is a
recipe for stress, frustration, condemnation, and needless pressure.

Jesus said, "If you love me, you will keep my commandments." Some will hear this through a filter of
condemnation that they need to prove their love by

being obedient. Take off those darkly-tinted goggles of guilt and put on God's prescription lenses of salvation, hope, and sanctification—you will see that love enables earnest obedience. God's commands aren't a list of rules to control you and weigh you down, they are guides to the holy path of righteousness. If you are feeling heavy, return to the Lord and refresh your first love. His love will give you strength and peace.

"My yoke is easy, and my burden is light."

MATTHEW 11:28

A WIFE–GOD'S GIFT

"A good wife is not found accidentally and without divine guidance. On the contrary, she is a gift of God and does not come, as the heathen imagine, in answer to our planning and judging."

Many Christians enter the dating pool with a list of qualifications for their potential spouse. They need to be dedicated to God, virtuous, prayerful, and know their Bible, among other godly traits. What more often trips us up is focusing on traits such as physical appearance, occupation, and salary. None of these things are inherently bad, but can create blindspots in your search for God's best for you.

Our perspective formed by our own genetic makeup, personality, upbringing, as well as our mental, physical, and spiritual diet, while it can be a blessing, can also be an inhibitor. We all have blindspots. This is just one reason that putting your search for a spouse in the hands of God and praying in faith for His best, will produce far better results than you could plan for. *"As the heavens are higher than the earth, so are my ways higher than your ways . . ."* says the Lord in Isaiah 55. If you are searching for a spouse, trust in God's timing and accept His divine guidance.

"Houses and wealth are inherited from parents, but a prudent wife is from the Lord."

PROVERBS 19:14 NIV

A PRAYER FOR STRENGTH

"Behold, Lord, here is an empty cask that needs to be filled. My Lord, fill it. I am weak in faith, strengthen me. I am cold in love; warm me and fill me with fire that my love may flow out over my neighbor."

I t is the testimony of many Christians that in dark times, when they found themselves at the end of their rope, they prayed to God for help and He answered. The circumstances of life and sinful nature can bring a person to their knees in acknowledgement that they need help.

Luther's prayer is a beautiful and humble petition to God, beginning with this essential recognition that we have a deep need for Him. We can return to our knees as we once did, confess our need for a Savior, and cry out to Him for strength. Return to Him again in your weakness, with faith that His grace is sufficient.

But he said to me, "My grace is sufficient for you, for my power is made perfect in weakness." Therefore I will boast all the more gladly about my weaknesses, so that Christ's power may rest on me. That is why, for Christ's sake, I delight in weaknesses, in insults, in hardships, in persecutions, in difficulties. For when I am weak, then I am strong.

2 CORINTHIANS 12:9-10 NIV

DID YOU KNOW

Luther had a life-long struggle with a condition he called *anfechtung,* a term he used to describe his experiences with doubt and temptation, his despair in his own sinfulness, and his terror that God was angry with him.

GIVING GENEROUSLY

"God divided the hand into fingers so that money would slip through."

In Matthew 19, after encountering a rich man in pursuit of eternal life, Jesus spoke to His disciples, *"Truly I tell you . . . it is easier for a camel to go through the eye of a needle than for someone who is rich to enter the kingdom of God." This was spoken after He instructed the man to give away all his possessions and follow him. Ultimately the man walked away sad, with scripture simply saying, "because he had great wealth."*

What Jesus is saying here is that wealth and possessions tether us to this world and make it harder to live for the next. It enables a standard of living that makes us feel secure in the number in our bank account, the size house we live in, the clothes we wear, or the cars we drive instead of finding our security in God. However, the Bible says it is the love of money that leads to all kinds of evil. All throughout scripture is instruction on using money as a tool to bless others and expand the kingdom of God.

Be a joyful steward of your temporary earthly resources. Generosity has an amazing conversion rate at the bank of heaven!

"Give, and it will be given to you . . . For whatever measure you deal out to others, it will be dealt to you in return."

LUKE 6:38 NASB

A POSITION OF HONOR

"No power on earth is so noble and so great as that of parents."

A parent is one of, if not the most impacting figure in an individuals life. A parent carries such immense power that they can start child off on a successful, fulfilling life or scar them with insecurity and trauma.

The decision to create life and invest your love, time, and resources into the next generation of human beings is a wonderful pursuit if pursued with intentionality—even more so as Christians. The Christian parent has the opportunity to create with God and understand new facets of God's role as our Father as they do.

If you are blessed to be a parent, ponder that the love that you feel for your child is only a glimmer of what your heavenly Father feels for you.

"Honor your father and mother"—which
is the first commandment with a
promise—"so that it may go well with you
and that you may enjoy long life on the
earth."

EPHESIANS 6:2-3 NIV

DID YOU KNOW

Martin Luther was born on November 10th, 1483 as
the eldest son to Hans and Margarethe Luther. Hans
owned copper mines and smelters, and served on the
local town council. Though he was a very strict
parent and was infuriated by Martin's decision to
abandon his education as a lawyer, Hans lived to see
Martin's success and fame as a reformer.

WORTHLESS RESERVES

"What sort of faith is that which trusts in God when all the while you feel and know that you have provisions in reserve by which you are able to help yourself?"

T rue faith shines brightest when we no longer lean on our own reserves. Martin Luther's words remind us that faith is not merely trusting God when the pantry is full, the savings secure, and the path clear—it's trusting Him when the cupboards feel bare and the road ahead uncertain. When we are at the end of our rope, that is when God moves in unforgettable ways and our faith shines brightest.

God invites us to rest in His sufficiency, not in our backup plans. As we loosen our grip on earthly securities, we discover His endless supply of grace, wisdom, and strength. Our faith grows strongest when it's stretched beyond our safety nets.

Some trust in chariots and some in horses, but we trust in the name of the Lord our God.

PSALM 20:7 NIV

DID YOU KNOW

Luther was kidnapped by a band of masked horsemen on his way home from Worms in 1521 and was hidden in Wartburg Castle for almost a year. Prince Frederick III of Saxony orchestrated this to protect him from the Edict of Worms that declared him an outlaw. It was here that Luther translated the New Testament from Greek into German.

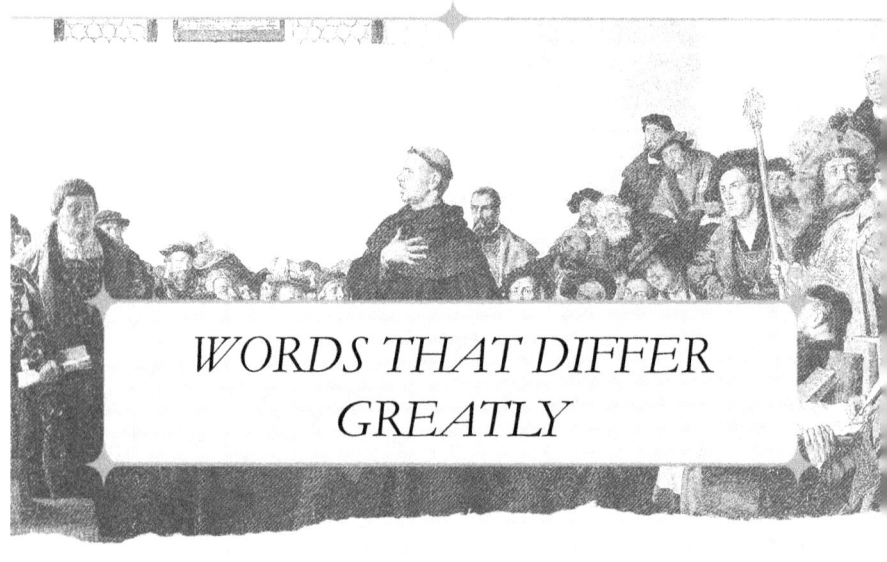

WORDS THAT DIFFER GREATLY

"We must make a great difference between God's Word and the word of man. A man's word is a little sound, that flies into the air, and soon vanishes; but the Word of God is greater than heaven and earth."

While there is much to be gleaned from the words of wise men, their wisdom only goes so deep. We are limited by our intellect, our finite understanding, and numerous sociological factors —but God's Word endures beyond time, standing firm when everything else shifts or crumbles. Scripture is not just ink on a page, but it is living, powerful, and eternal.

When we anchor our hearts in God's promises rather than in the opinions of others, we find a foundation that cannot be shaken.

Today, ask yourself: whose words carry the most weight in your heart? Let God's unchanging Word be your compass and the steady hope for your soul.

There is a way which seemeth right unto a man, but the end thereof are the ways of death.

PROVERBS 14:12

DID YOU KNOW

In 1517, Luther famously nailed a list of scholarly objections to church practices to the doors of All Saints' Church in Wittenberg. This story is based more on legend than verified truth. In reality, Luther wrote to his bishop Albrecht von Brandenburg with a copy of his "Disputation on the Power and Efficacy of Indulgences", which later became known as the Ninety-Five Theses.

CHILDREN–
GOD'S CREATION

"Daily learn the article of divine creation by looking at your children and offspring, who stand before you . . . Here you may behold the providence of God, who created them out of nothing."

Martin Luther invites us to witness God's hand in the most familiar of places: our family. Each child's laughter and curious eyes are living reminders that God brings forth life where there once was nothing.

Too often we overlook these daily miracles, rushing past the ordinary that testifies to divine power. When we pause to truly see, our hearts are stirred with gratitude and wonder for the Creator who still sustains all things.

Take a moment to marvel at the life around you. Whether in children, nature, or new beginnings, let it remind you that the same God who creates also cares for you.

"Lo, children are an heritage from the
Lord: and the fruit of the womb is his
reward."

PSALM 127:3

DID YOU KNOW

Luther married Katharina von Bora in 1525, an ex-
nun whom he helped escape from a convent during
the early Reformation. Together they had six children
and raised four orphaned children.

THE LIVING WORD

"The Bible is alive, it speaks to me; it has feet, it runs after me; it has hands, it lays hold of me."

How many times have you reread familiar passages, and a verse hits you like you had never read it before? That is because the Bible is not simply a book, a compilation of men's imaginative writings and wisdom—it's alive with the spirit of God.

Scripture speaks directly to our hearts, guiding, correcting, and comforting us in ways no other words can. When life feels overwhelming or lonely, God's Word lays hold of us, steadying our steps and drawing us back to His truth.

Open your Bible with fresh eyes and expect it to speak life to you. God Himself is reaching out to you through its pages.

For the word of God is alive and active.
Sharper than any double-edged sword, it
penetrates even to dividing soul and spirit,
joints and marrow; it judges the thoughts
and attitudes of the heart.

HEBREWS 4:12 NIV

DID YOU KNOW

Luther said this at the Diet held in the imperial city
of Worms: "Unless I am convinced by the testimony
of the Scriptures or by clear reason … I am bound
by the Scriptures that I have quoted and my
conscience is captive to the Word of God. I cannot
and I will not retract anything, since it is neither safe
nor right to go against conscience."

WATCHING OVER CHILDREN

"The dear angels are not so proud as we human beings are. They walk in obedience to God, serve mankind, and take care of little children. How could they perform a more insignificant work than taking care of children day and night?"

L uther's reflection reminds us that true greatness is found in humble service. Angels, majestic and heavenly beings, do not consider it beneath them to watch over children or protect those who cannot protect themselves. If such glorious creatures find joy in serving quietly and faithfully, how much more should we embrace humility in our own lives?

God calls us to serve others with the same obedience and willingness. Every small act of kindness, every moment of patient care, carries eternal significance.

Ask God to help you lay aside pride and serve with the gentle humility of the angels, knowing that in doing so, you are fulfilling a holy mission from God.

For he will command his angels
concerning you to guard you in all your
ways; they will lift you up in their
hands, so that you will not strike your foot
against a stone.

PSALM 91:11-12 NIV

DID YOU KNOW

Luther was forty-two when he became a father. He
wrote letters to his children during the many times he
was away from home; sometimes he even took them
with him on his journeys. At home, he would play
and make music with them.

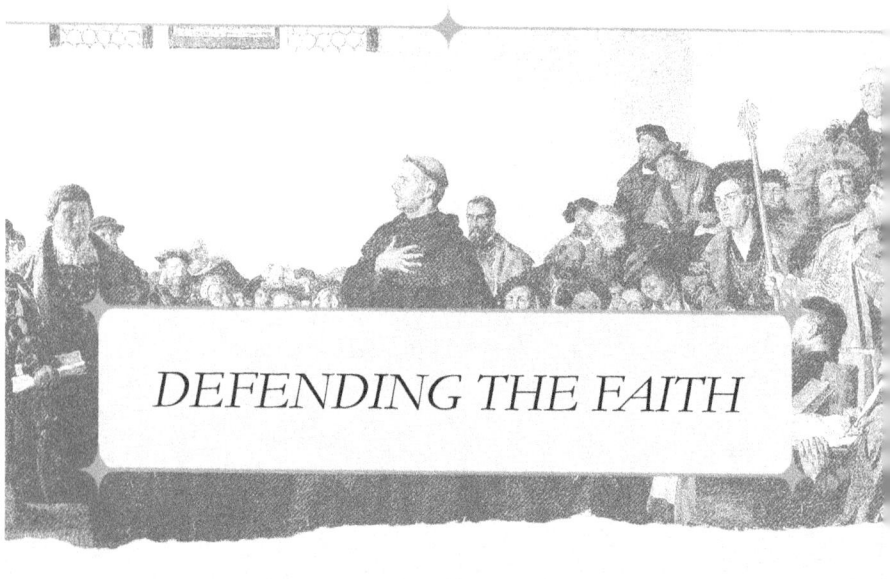

DEFENDING THE FAITH

"Here stand I. I can do no other. God help me. Amen."

S ofia sat in the break room, listening as her coworkers debated faith with mocking laughter. Her heart pounded—she wanted to speak up, but feared rejection. She was not the bold type nor particularly well-spoken, but she could not ignore the nudge in her chest to say something.

Whispering a prayer under her breath, she gently shared how her faith had given her hope during hard times. The room grew quiet. Instead of offense, she was met with thoughtful questions. One coworker approached her later, admitting she was also a Christian who struggled to share her faith, and said her boldness had inspired her to be more vocal.

Like Sofia, we may feel unequipped to witness at work, but God supplies courage. When the moment comes to stand for Christ, remember the valiant stand Luther made and the cloud of witnesses cheering you on. You never know who desperately needs the hope you have in Christ.

Blessed are they which are persecuted for righteousness' sake: for theirs is the kingdom of heaven.

MATTHEW 5:10

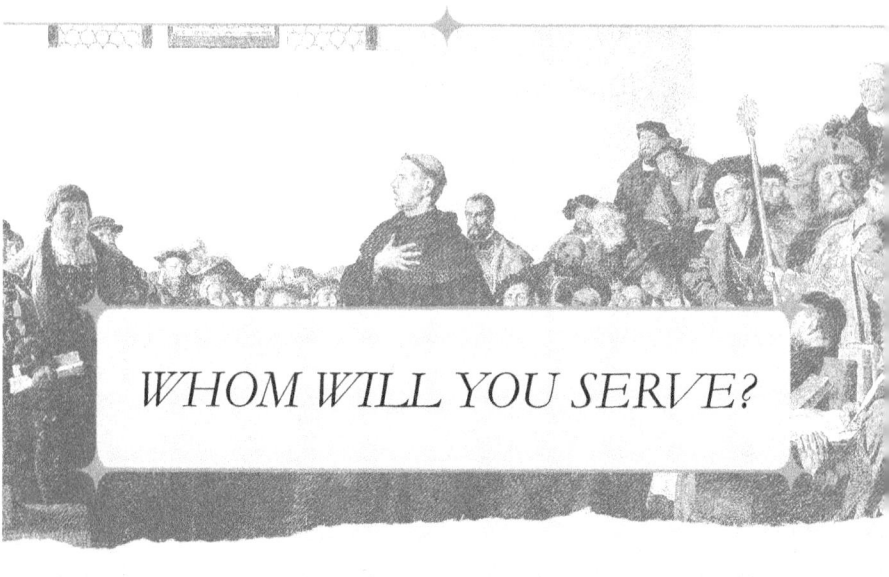

WHOM WILL YOU SERVE?

"Whatever your heart clings to and confides in, that is really your God."

Success, relationships, money, approval—these can be great things, but when they become our source of security, they can quietly take God's place. Everyone builds a totem pole in their minds and hearts, often subconsciously, where we sort people and achievements in order of personal importance. Whatever we place at the top has the greatest influence on our daily sense of purpose and attitude. Only the Lord is worthy of the greatest place in our hearts and produces lasting joy and peace in our lives—anything or anyone else will fall short. Psalm 62:8 urges us, *"Trust in Him at all times... pour out your hearts to Him, for God is our refuge."*

Take a moment to ask yourself: what makes up the "totem pole" in your life, and where does God land on it? Choose to make God the king of your heart. He will not fail you when everything else falters.

For where your treasure is, there your
heart will be also.

MATTHEW 6:21 NIV

KEEP THE WOLVES AT BAY

"An upright shepherd and minister must improve his flock by edification, and also resist and defend it; otherwise, if resisting be absent, the wolf devours the sheep."

True shepherding requires both gentle care and bold resistance. A shepherd who only feeds the sheep but never guards them leaves the flock vulnerable to the lurking wolf. In Bible times, shepherds often slept at the entrance of the sheepfold at night, guarding the door from predators.

In our own lives, whether as parents, leaders, or friends, we are called to build others up with encouragement and truth. Sometimes that entails speaking up and standing firm against lies, temptations, or harmful influences. Jesus, our Good Shepherd, both nurtures us and defends us from the enemy's schemes. Extend this same resolve as you watch over those under your care.

Keep watch over yourselves and all the flock of which the Holy Spirit has made you overseers. Be shepherds of the church of God, which he bought with his own blood. I know that after I leave, savage wolves will come in among you and will not spare the flock.

ACTS 20:28-29 NIV

DID YOU KNOW

Luther was convinced that the devil uses many devices to ruin to the church, one of his most lethal being when God's people act like he doesn't exist. While some of Luther's ideas about the devil were influenced by medieval superstition, he experienced how the devil tried to instill doubt God's promises and question the certainty of his salvation.

JUSTIFIED FOR WORKS

"He who is justified performs good works; for this is the meaning of Scripture: Justification precedes good works, and works are performed by those who are justified."

I t is a common misconception that one must "clean up" before we approach God or begin attending church. When we play into this belief, we allow the shame we feel for our sin to overshadow the gospel. In truth, no amount of "getting our life together" will make us worthy of His grace—it is the sacrifice of Jesus alone that qualifies us. We're not saved by what we do, but by what Christ has already done.

Once we receive His free gift of salvation and grace, something shifts in our hearts. We are transformed in the presence of God and kindness, generosity, and service grow from the overflow of our heart. Instead of striving to "be a good person", we can rest in the assurance of justification and allow our works to spring forth as a joyful response to the grace we've already been given.

"For we are his workmanship, created in Christ Jesus unto good works, which God hath before ordained that we should walk in them."

EPHESIANS 2:10

DEVILS ON THE ROOF

"If I heard that as many devils would set on me in Worms as there are tiles on the roofs, I should nonetheless have ridden there."

Luther knew the risks of standing for truth, yet he chose to ride into Worms, trusting God more than his fears. He faced threats to his life and his livelihood in doing so, and yet he considered the weight of conviction he carried to be worth it all.

We, too, face moments when opposition feels overwhelming. Whether it's criticism, doubt, or the weight of circumstances, we can take heart knowing that the same God who sustained Luther rides with us. As Romans 8:31 says, *"If God is for us, who can be against us?"*

When the path ahead appears lined with obstacles,

MARTIN LUTHER'S Little Instruction Book

remember that God goes before you, watches behind you, and is walking alongside you. Walk in step with Him.

Submit yourselves therefore to God.
Resist the devil, and he will flee from you.

JAMES 4:7

GOD'S REPRESENTATIVES

"We must train young people to look upon their parents as God's representatives and to remember that even thought they are lowly, poor, frail, and peculiar, they are still the father and mother whom God gave them."

When Sarah moved back home to care for her aging father, old wounds resurfaced. She remembered his stern words and her mother's controlling habits that she would've given anything to escape from in her teen years.

Yet one evening, as she watched her father struggle to open a jar with trembling hands, her heart softened. She was now in the role of caregiver, as he was similarly when she was unable to care for herself. With all their flaws, they successfully raised her into a thriving adult. She gently took the jar and cracked it open, handing it back to him with a grateful smile.

Ephesians 6:2 calls us to *"honor your father and*

mother," not because they are perfect, but because God entrusted them to us. Find peace by extending the same grace to your parents that Christ extended to you.

Honour thy father and thy mother: that thy days may be long upon the land which the Lord thy God giveth thee.

EXODUS 20:12

SPIRITUAL PRIDE

"Reason cannot break itself of this habit: if it finds itself favored by God before others, it must turn up its nose at those who do not enjoy such favor."

When blessings flow, it's tempting to believe we've somehow earned more of God's favor than others. We get a big promotion or gain financial success, and glorify ourselves as "self-made" rather than pointing to the Lord.

Scripture reminds us in James 1:17 that *"every good and perfect gift is from above."* God's blessings are not badges of superiority but invitations to gratitude and service. True humility celebrates God's goodness without comparison and extends compassion to those still waiting for their breakthrough.

Ask the Lord to guard your heart from pride and let every instance of God's favor become an opportunity to glorify Him.

God chose the lowly things of this world
and the despised things—and the things
that are not—to nullify the things that
are, so that no one may boast before him.

1 CORINTHIANS 1:28-29 NIV

DID YOU KNOW

Luther was not alone in his work, often collaborating
with Philipp Melanchthon, Johannes Bugenhagen,
and more on projects. In the preface to the 1529
German translation of Melanchthon's commentary
of Colossians, Luther described himself as the rough
woodsman, clearing the forest so that Melanchthon
could follow as the happy farmer, planting crops.

BLINDED BY THE LIGHT

"Blessed is he who delights in [the Word of God] and gladly see this light, for it loves to shine. But moles and bats, that is, the people of the world, do not like it."

The world often prefers the shadows because the light exposes what needs to change. At one time in your life, you may have found yourself stumbling through life, as if on a moonless night, looking for purpose and peace. In the shadows, all we see are silhouettes and vague shapes of what lies in front of us.

Psalm 119:105 says, *"Your word is a lamp to my feet and a light to my path."* God's Word reveals truth, comforts our hearts, and guides our steps, but only if we're willing to open our eyes to it. When we delight in Scripture, we invite the light of God to transform us from within.

Choose to step into God's light with joy today, letting His Word illuminate every corner of your life. It might sting a little, like opening curtains first thing in the morning, but there is freedom waiting on the other side.

He that loveth his brother abideth in the light, and there is none occasion of stumbling in him.

1 JOHN 2:10

TOO VAST TO
UNDERSTAND

"I shall need to have been dead several years before I shall thoroughly understand the meaning of creation and the omnipotence of God."

Martin Luther shares a sentiment you can probably relate to: the mystery of God. Creation itself whispers of His infinite power in incredible mountain peaks and valleys, babbling brooks in lush forests, and the gentle fall of snow. Yet even with all our learning, we only glimpse a fraction of His majesty. God's greatness stretches far beyond what our minds can grasp.

As Ecclesiastes 3:11 says, *"He has made everything beautiful in its time. He has also set eternity in the human heart; yet no one can fathom what God has done."* One day, in eternity, we'll see clearly the wonder we can now only stand in awe of. We don't need to understand everything to trust the One who does. Faith invites us to rest in what we cannot fully explain, knowing we are in the capable and caring hands of the Almighty God.

Can you fathom the mysteries of God?
Can you probe the limits of the Almighty?
They are higher than the heavens above—
what can you do? They are deeper than
the depths below—what can you know?

JOB 11:7-8 NIV

A PENITENT HEART

"A penitent heart is a rare thing and a great grace; one cannot produce it by thinking about sin and hell. Only the Holy Spirit can impart it."

E llen sat alone as congregants started filing into a Sunday morning service. She stared up at the large cross displayed on the stage, dappled in multicolor light shimmering through the stained glass. An icon that brought many comfort and inspiration made her stomach churn. Ellen was raised by her grandmother, who scared her into nightly prayers with talks of hell and sin. Years of begging for forgiveness from whom she believed to be an angry God resulted in church fading from her life by adulthood.

But something had drawn her back today. She felt old pangs of shame coming back, and she began to kick herself for coming. Then, the choir began to softly sing

"Amazing Grace." Tears began to fall. The simple words suddenly hit her like she had never heard them before, and she felt the warmth of mercy pour over her. It wasn't guilt that broke her; it was love. From then on, Ellen learned repentance wasn't about earning forgiveness, but it was a miraculous gift to be received. And for the first time, she felt seen and loved.

"Search me, O God, and know my heart:
try me, and know my thoughts: And see if
there be any wicked way in me, and lead
me in the way everlasting."

PSALM 139:24

THE BARKING DOG
OF REGRET

"Regret, the little black dog of a belated repentance, does not stop barking and biting the conscience, even though you know that your sins are forgiven."

Anyone who has lived a life of sin before coming to God knows this feeling well. When you look back at the past as years wasted, it's very easy to fall into a trap of regret and shame. You're now living for God and know you're forgiven, yet the unease lingers. Martin Luther understood this tug-of-war between grace and guilt.

When regret growls, remember that feelings don't define forgiveness. Christ's sacrifice was enough, once and for all. You don't need to silence the barking, you only need tune in to the Shepherd's voice that calls you beloved and free. Let His mercy drown out the noise. Grace doesn't erase the past—it redeems it, one quiet moment of trust at a time.

Godly sorrow brings repentance that
leads to salvation and leaves no regret, but
worldly sorrow brings death.

2 CORINTHIANS 7:10 NIV

DID YOU KNOW

Luther insisted that Christians are righteous and sinner
at the same time (*"simul iustus et peccator"*). He was not
giving believers an excuse to sin, but was providing a
way to be honest about themselves and about God's
mercy. While translating the Bible, Luther became
convinced that the word in the Greek New Testament
translated as "grace" (*charis*) did not designate a power
dwelling in us, but God's unmerited mercy.

BELIEVE IN THE SON!

"It is the will and pleasure of the Father that he who sees the Son and believes in Him have eternal life. Would to God this fact would sink into the heart! If only people would think what this means!"

Martin Luther longed for this truth to sink deep into our hearts: the Father's will is that everyone who sees and believes in the Son will have eternal life.

This is the basic gospel, one many of us can recite from Sunday school, and part of a prayer we prayed when we first got saved. But imagine if we lived every day with that awareness, not just as a distant promise, but as a present reality shaping how we speak, forgive, and hope. Eternal life doesn't begin when we die, it begins when faith opens our eyes.

Today, pause and let that truth settle in: God's will is not against you. His desire is that you *live* fully and joyfully through His Son today and every day. What peace would you carry if you truly believed that?

For I am convinced that neither death nor life, neither angels nor demons, neither the present nor the future, nor any powers, neither height nor depth, nor anything else in all creation, will be able to separate us from the love of God that is in Christ Jesus our Lord.

ROMANS 8:38-39 NIV

DID YOU KNOW.

Luther's "theology of the cross" was not a theory about the cross alone, but the belief that God always reveals himself in the last place human beings would reasonably look: with the Israelites not the Egyptians; in a manger; on the cross; among mortal sinners in the church.

THE GREATEST PURIFIER

"A fiery shield is God's Word; of more substance and purer than gold, which, tried in the fire, loses nought of its substance."

G old, when refined by fire, sheds its impurities. The more refined, the more valuable the gold. But the Word of God is both the most valuable gold and the hottest fire, its words both pure and capable of purifying. It is gentle enough to warm cold hearts, and yet burns with an intensity no sin can hide from.

When trials blaze around you, this shield does not melt. It glows brighter yet, defending your heart and strengthening your faith. Every promise and every truth stands the heat of battle and the test of time. Hold fast to Scripture when the world feels like it is melting down. When everything else burns up in fiery trials, the Word of God will remain faithful and true companion.

But he said, Yea rather, blessed are they
that hear the word of God, and keep it.

LUKE 11:28

DID YOU KNOW

Luther translated New Testament in 1522 and the
full Bible 1534. What differentiated his translations
from other German versions at the time was his
idiomatic approach that prioritized adapting it
phrase-by-phrase rather than word-by-word. This
resulted in a more linguistically digestible translation,
albeit at the expense of accuracy by some standards.

FREEDOM TO SERVE

"A Christian is a free lord of all and subject to no one. A Christian is a ministering servant of all and subject to everyone."

Martin Luther captured the beautiful paradox of faith: the Christian is both utterly free and humbly bound. In Christ, we are freed from the impossible burden of earning God's favor and free from the slavery of sin. Yet this same freedom calls us to obey and serve with the humility Jesus displayed.

True liberty is found not in self-rule, but in self-giving. When we stoop to wash another's feet, offer forgiveness, or lend a hand without expecting reward, we live out the heart of Jesus. Freedom through Christ is freedom from self-preservation and self-importance that would have us withhold good from others. Give freely and generously of whatever resources you've been blessed with, and you will know the provision of God to thrive beyond your capacity.

Though I am free and belong to no one, I have made myself a slave to everyone, to win as many as possible.

1 CORINTHIANS 9:19 NIV

LOVING THE RASCALS

*"Our Lord God must be a pious man to be able to love
rascals. I can't do it and yet I am a rascal myself."*

L uther's honest and humorous observation
speaks to the everyday reality of the Christian. We stumble, lose our tempers, make selfish choices, and fall short daily. Yet God doesn't with-
draw His love, He leans in closer. His mercy isn't based
on our performance, but on His perfect nature.

Even though we know and benefit from this, it can
still be hard to extend the same grace to others. When we
practice meditation on the goodness and grace of God,
humility takes root and judgment fades. We start seeing
others not as "rascals" to endure, but as souls just as loved
and forgiven as we are. Let gratitude move you to extend
that same patient grace, from one rascal to another.

A new commandment I give unto you,
That ye love one another; as I have loved
you, that ye also love one another. By this
shall all men know that ye are my
disciples, if ye have love one to another.

JOHN 13:34-35

DID YOU KNOW

Johann Tetzel, a Dominican friar, was sent to
Germany in 1516 by the Roman Catholic Church to
sell indulgences to raise money to rebuild St. Peter's
Basilica in Rome. His preaching that souls could be
sprung from purgatory by purchasing indulgences
was what spurred Luther to write to his bishop,
enclosing a letter that would later be known as the
the Ninety-Five Theses.

HE BORE
OUR PUNISHMENT

"Christ is the One who stepped into the place of our sinful nature, loaded upon Himself, and appeased for us all, the wrath of God which we had deserved by all our works."

The staggering exchange of sin and salvation is the heart of the gospel. Christ stepped into our place, carrying the full weight of sin we could never bear. He didn't wait for us to deserve it, but He bore our guilt willingly, absorbing every ounce of wrath that justice required.

When guilt or shame whisper that you've fallen too far from grace to be redeemed, remember Jesus already went farther. He took your place so you could stand before the throne of God with confidence. Rest in that grace today and live not from guilt, but from gratitude for the One who made you free.

Since we have now been justified by his blood, how much more shall we be saved from God's wrath through him! For if, while we were God's enemies, we were reconciled to him through the death of his Son, how much more, having been reconciled, shall we be saved through his life!

ROMANS 5:9-10 NIV

DID YOU KNOW

Luther insisted that, since forgiveness was God's alone to grant, claiming indulgences absolved buyers from punishment and granted them salvation were in serious error. He called out the sale of indulgences in his eighty-sixth thesis: "Why does the pope, whose wealth today is greater than the wealth of the richest Crassus, build the basilica of St. Peter with the money of poor believers . . .?"

FREE WILL IS SELF WILL

"I wish that the expression 'free will' had never been invented. It is not recorded in Scripture either and should more justly be called self-will, which is worthless."

When Daniel was offered a promotion that promised wealth but required quiet compromise, he felt the tension between right and wrong. Success was waiting on the other side of signing a contract that contradicted his personal beliefs. There were a hundred reasons to accept, a million ways his life and that of his family would benefit. His pride said, *You deserve this.* His spirit whispered, *But at what cost?*

When we follow our desires apart from God, it leads us down a path that may appear pleasant at first, but promises regret. Daniel turned down the offer with, knowing true freedom is found in following the ways of God, not his own way. Each day, we stand at the same crossroads: our will or God's. When we surrender self-will, we don't lose freedom, but we finally discover it in the One whose will leads to life.

The mind governed by the flesh is hostile to God; it does not submit to God's law, nor can it do so.

ROMANS 8:7 NIV

NO MORE BOOKS

"I would indeed consent to have all my books perish; for I have sought nothing with them but to bring to light Holy Scripture and the divine truth."

I n a world obsessed with leaving legacies and clouded by ego, Luther's words call us to refocus on the heart of why we do what we do. Though he was a prolific author, using the written word to share the truth of God's word and the convictions he had in the process, his priorities were straight. It's not about the material he created, or building legacy or fame, it's about the message.

Our words, accomplishments, and possessions will fade, but God's Word remains living and eternal. When the wisdom that parents pass onto their children is rooted in scripture, something deeper is planted than fond memories. When we seek to point others toward

Him rather than ourselves, our impact multiplies far beyond our lifetime.

Ask yourself: are you striving to be remembered, or to help others remember God? True legacy is not in what bears our name, but in what bears His truth.

For the Lord giveth wisdom: out of his mouth cometh knowledge and understanding.

PROVERBS 2:6

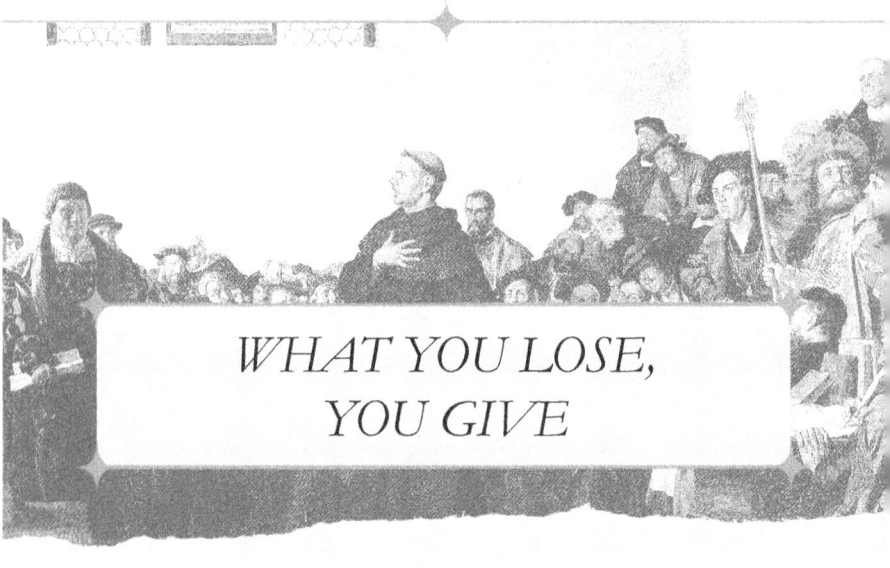

WHAT YOU LOSE,
YOU GIVE

"For whatever your injury and loss of temporal possessions may be, they are, in these circumstances, sacrifices offered to Christ Himself."

W hen Anna's small bakery burned down from an unnoticed gas leak, she felt as though her dreams had literally turned to ashes. Years of work gone overnight. As she sifted through the charred remains, a deep ache filled her chest. She whispered a prayer: "Lord, this was always Yours. If it is your will, you can breathe new life into these ashes." In the quiet of loss, there was a seedling of hope planted in her.

Her grief watered the soil of her heart, and over time that seedling grew. She began baking again—this time not for profit, but to feed the hungry in her community. What once felt like loss became an offering.

Martin Luther's words remind us that even our suffering can become sacred when given to Christ. Every loss surrendered to Him is transformed into worship, and every wound becomes a place for His healing glory to shine.

"And everyone who has left houses or brothers or sisters or father or mother or children or fields for my sake will receive a hundred times as much and will inherit eternal life."

MATTHEW 19:29 NIV

A PURE HEART

"No one is better prepared for Judgment Day than the person who longs to be without sin."

You needn't take more than one look at the news, one scroll through social media, or one walk downtown to know this world is corrupt. There are times when the world around us produces a deep longing within for the next life. This longing isn't born from fear, but from love for the One who redeems what is out of order. As Jesus declares in his sermon on the Mount of Olives, *"The pure of heart shall see God."* The one who truly longs to be without sin has already found a crucial ingredient to taste heaven on earth.

Luther reiterates that a heart eager for purity is a heart already turned toward God. Such a person doesn't pretend perfection, but humbly admits their need for grace. Each confession, each instance of repentance, is a step closer to the light. On Judgment Day, it won't be spotless lives that stand secure, but it will be surrendered hearts clothed in Christ's righteousness who rejoice to be restored and made whole in the glory of God.

"Create in me a clean heart, O God; and
renew a right spirit within me."

PSALM 51:10

THE GREATEST OF THESE IS . . .

"Patience, chasteness, moderation, etc. are fine virtues, too; but they are trivial when compared with love, which includes all other virtues and brings them in its train."

Paul famously elaborates on this in 1 Corinthians 13, listing a variety of honorable and even godly things that are rendered useless if devoid of love. Patience can calm storms, chasteness can purify our motives, and moderation can steady our steps, but all of them make up an incomplete picture without love.

When love fills the heart, patience occurs naturally, kindness becomes effortless, and humility finds its place. Without love, even our best deeds lose their power. True love—the kind that reflects Christ—does not seek its own glory but pours itself out for others. When we walk in love, we don't have to strive to be virtuous, love itself shapes us into the likeness of the One who is love Himself.

"If I give all I possess to the poor and surrender my body to the flames, but have not love, I gain nothing."

1 CORINTHIANS 13:3 NIV

DID YOU KNOW

Foundational to the Luthers' home life was his wife, Katharina von Bora, whom he lovingly called Katie. She not only cared for their children and home, but also told Luther straight if his talk was too full of animosity.

UNEXPECTED REWARDS

"It is impossible that reward should not follow when we seek God in a purely selfless spirit, without any expectation of reward and advantage."

Luther's words here challenge the hidden motives of the heart. How often do we serve God with a quiet hope that He'll bless us in return, answer our prayers, bestow favor, or bring us peace? Luther reminds us that true devotion seeks God, not gain.

Even though God Himself is the reward, when we correct our human instinct for a transactional relationship, God fills our hands anyway. After all, He is a good Father who delights to give good things to His children. The heart that seeks Him selflessly becomes the heart most deeply satisfied. Seek Him for who He is, not what He gives, and you'll gain everything that matters and more.

"He is a rewarder of them that diligently seek him."

HEBREWS 11:6

DID YOU KNOW

Though Luther gained a great amount of fame during his lifetime, he lived very modestly, if not at a level of poverty. He wrote to a collegue in 1525, "My Katie is in all things so obliging and pleasing to me that I would not exchange my poverty for the riches of Croesus."

WRATH AND MERCY

"The wrath of God is real, not fictitious, not a jest. If it were false, then mercy would be fictitious; for as the wrath, so the mercy which forgives . . ."

L uther's statement is a sobering truth. We cannot grasp the depth of God's mercy without first understanding the reality of His wrath. In a world that prefers comfort over conviction, it's tempting to downplay sin and imagine God's judgment as symbolic. Very few want to appeal to non-believers with the fire of Hell out of fear of scaring people away or even labeling the judgment of God as problematic. But if wrath were not real, neither would mercy be meaningful.

The cross of Christ proves both. God's holiness demanded justice, yet His love provided the sacrifice. The nails that pierced Jesus were not just symbols, but they were the price of mercy paid in full. Let us not run from the truth of God's wrath, but through it, run straight into the arms of His redeeming love with new depths of gratitude and understanding.

Put to death, therefore, whatever belongs to your earthly nature: sexual immorality, impurity, lust, evil desires and greed, which is idolatry. Because of these, the wrath of God is coming.

COLOSSIANS 3:5-6 NIV

CRAWLING TOWARD HEAVEN

"Why, then, am I, when my soul's salvation is concerned, so sluggish and sleepy that God must drag me to it by the very hair? Why, I ought to spit at myself for not even crawling to heaven while those folk rush and run to hell the way they do."

How often we have a harder time choosing what is good for us over what is not. Kids grimace at spinach and rush for candy, we "snooze" ourselves late for work, or we waste time scrolling endlessly on our phones while we postpone time with God. We chase comfort and pleasure with passion, yet when it comes to the salvation of our souls, we often grow weary, distracted, or indifferent.

Luther's raw confession reminds us that spiritual laziness isn't harmless, but it's a subtle drift away from living life as God intended for us. When we lose sight of eternal perspective, precious time slips through our fingers like sand, believing there is always tomorrow when tomorrow is not guaranteed. God shouldn't have to drag us toward His grace, yet He often does, because His love refuses to let us go. Today, let's awaken our faith. Let us run toward heaven, stirred by gratitude and not guilt.

... Forgetting what is behind and straining toward what is ahead, I press on toward the goal to win the prize for which God has called me heavenward in Christ Jesus.

PHILIPPIANS 3:13-14 NIV

WHEN WORK IS SIN

"To want to merit grace by works which precede faith is to want to appease God by sins."

By all outward appearances, Toby was a gold-star Christian. He volunteered, read his bible every day, gave generously, and never missed a Sunday service. Yet deep down, his heart was restless. Secretly, he prided himself as superior because he excelled above the Christians around him by the volume of his good deeds.

One morning at an outreach event, his pastor shared the gospel and a lightning bolt of revelation hit Toby. He had been living out of the belief that it was his actions that earned God's love and favor, as if his good works could erase his sin. He had forgotten the heart of his faith: the gospel.

Toby knelt down in his room that night and repented for his pride. His good works didn't vanish, but they became expressions of gratitude, not transactions for mercy. He realized grace isn't achieved—it's accepted.

If, in fact, Abraham was justified by works, he had something to boast about—but not before God. What does Scripture say? "Abraham believed God, and it was credited to him as righteousness."

ROMANS 4:2-3 NIV

HANDLING POSSESSIONS

"Possessions are not given that we may rely on them and glory in them . . . but that we may use and enjoy them and share them with others . . . Our possessions should be in our hands, not in our hearts."

I t's so easy in the day-to-day bustle of life to lose sight of the life to come. Too often we hold our money, time, or talents so tightly that they begin to hold us. But God never intended blessings to be trophies sitting on our shelves collecting dust. He entrusts us with what we have so we can use it freely, enjoy it with gratitude, and share it generously.

When possessions find their place in our hands rather than our hearts, they become tools instead of idols. A backyard grill becomes a catalyst for neighborhood evangelism, a large home becomes a hub for hospitality, or a budget surplus becomes provision for someone in need. After all, the blessings we enjoy in this life come from the Lord. Remembering to whom all things belong helps us to loosen our grip, and we can make space for peace, contentment, and purpose. God's richest blessings flow through open hands.

"I tell you, use worldly wealth to gain friends for yourselves, so that when it is gone, you will be welcomed into eternal dwellings. Whoever can be trusted with very little can also be trusted with much, and whoever is dishonest with very little will also be dishonest with much."

LUKE 16:9-10 NIV

TO GOSSIPS AND SLANDERERS

"If you were his friend, you would keep silent and not circulate the misfortune of your neighbor with such pleasure and delight. In fact, you would convert your displeasure into pity and mercy."

I t's not uncommon to slip into the habit of sharing someone else's mistakes or exposing vulnerability shared in confidence under the guise of concern. How quickly a prayer request can twist into a gossip session. But Luther reminds us that true, godly friendship chooses compassion and protection over gossip.

When we take delight in another's downfall, even secretly, we reveal more about our own heart than theirs. God calls us instead to cover others in grace, to turn judgment into mercy, and criticism into prayer. Imagine the healing that would follow if every whispered story became an intercession instead. Silence is

MARTIN LUTHER'S Little Instruction Book

not always weakness—sometimes it is wisdom. When you choose pity over pleasure in another's misfortune, you reflect the heart of a Savior who covered your deepest faults with His mercy.

"It is the glory of God to conceal a matter."

PROVERBS 25:2 NIV

A BIG SNOWBALL

"A lie is like a snowball. The longer it is rolled on the ground, the larger it becomes."

W hen Ethan was applying to a prestigious position at an advertising firm in the city, he found his resume to be lackluster. So he fudged some numbers, added a few more years experience than he actually had, and threw in that he was fluent in Mandarin. When he got the interview, he carefully selected his outfit as he rehearsed an exchange in Mandarin, to feign authenticity in case they asked. Ethan got the job and thrived in it, until he was given a special client from China. Stress built up, but he was able to manage by communicating strictly over email where he could use google translate.

Ethan thought he was going to drop dead from a

heart attack when he arrived at work to be greeted by his Chinese client waiting in his office. His assistant had forgotten to book the meeting in his calendar. What followed was the most humiliating moment of his life and a breach of trust that cost him his job.

Luther's words remind us that deceit is a web that eventually entangles the weaver. Truth may cost us comfort, but the destruction a lie can cause carries a much heavier cost.

He that covereth his sins shall not prosper: but whoso confesseth and forsaketh them shall have mercy.

PROVERBS 28:13

THE DANGER OF PRIDE

"It is a particularly perilous task not to turn proud but to remain humble if God graces a person with outstanding, splendid talents."

S uccess has a strange way of testing the heart. When God blesses us with gifts, creativity, leadership, or skill, it's easy to start believing those abilities came from our own hands. Pride slips in quietly, whispering that we are self-made.

Luther emphasizes that the greater the gift, the greater the need for humility. Every talent is a trust from God, meant to bring glory to Him rather than ourselves. True greatness is not in being admired, but in using what we've been given to uplift others. The moment we start taking credit for God's grace, we lose sight of its source. Stay low before Him, and He will lift you higher than pride ever could.

A man's pride shall bring him low: but
honour shall uphold the humble in spirit.

PROVERBS 29:23

DID YOU KNOW

Luther's early education, cast aside when he choose
to abandon it for life in a monastery, did play an
important role in his rise as a reformer. He could talk
and write on the level of a learned scholar, but also
tell stories young children could understand. He was
feared by enemies and praised by friends for his great
skill in speech.

SECRET OF CONTENTMENT

"Now he who . . . knows that we are all equal in Christ goes about his work with delight and is not concerned even though for this short time here on earth he is in more modest circumstances and in a lowlier position than another."

The world measures worth by titles, possessions, appearance, and power, but the kingdom of God measures differently. While earthly favor can be a tool, more often than not it can be a slippery slope into pride and distraction. Your value is not found in status, but in the Savior who redeemed you. When our hearts find rest in that truth, even humble work becomes holy work.

Luther himself found great fame in his time and beyond. Though he very well could have taken advantage of this and built a wealthy life, he lived modestly, sharing his home and his work with his community.

The believer who knows they are equal in Christ

serves with joy, content to labor faithfully where God has placed them. In eternity, earthly ranks fade, and only love and glory remain. So whether you're sweeping floors, running your own business, or cleaning up after your young children, do your work with delight. Know that Heaven smiles down on your life lived for Him, whatever value the world places on it.

For we brought nothing into the world, and we can take nothing out of it. But if we have food and clothing, we will be content with that.

1 TIMOTHY 6:7-8 NIV

KNOWING
BY EXPERIENCE

"No one understands Scripture unless it is brought home to him, that is, unless he experiences it."

S arah sat in her car with her friend, tears streaking her face after receiving news she didn't know how to bear. Sarah was struggling to find the words to comfort her friend—what could possibly alleviate the pain she was feeling?

Then, through the fog of grief, a verse she'd memorized years ago surfaced: *"The Lord is close to the brokenhearted and saves those who are crushed in spirit."* She had read it before, perhaps even highlighted it, but now she finally felt it. Sarah shared the verse from her heart with her friend and the peace of God washed over them. In that moment, the words weren't distant or poetic, they were alive. It didn't change her circumstances, but it gave her friend the hope she needed to move forward.

That day was the beginning of a new appetite for God's Word in Sarah's life. From that day on, the verses she read weren't just words, but living promises of wisdom, peace, and hope.

For everything that was written in the past was written to teach us, so that through the endurance taught in the Scriptures and the encouragement they provide we might have hope.

ROMANS 15:4 NIV

FAITH AND LOVE
WORKING TOGETHER

"Faith receives the good works of Christ;
love does good works for the neighbor."

F aith and love walk hand in hand, yet they
play their own key roles. Faith is the open
hand that receives all Christ has done: His
mercy, His righteousness, His finished work on the
cross. Love, in turn, is the hand that gives, pouring out
what faith has received. Faith anchors us in grace, while
love drives us to share the hope we've found.

When you forgive someone who hurt you, comfort
the weary, or serve without expecting return, you are
letting the love of Christ overflow through you. Faith
fills the vessel of our heart and love empties it for the
good of another. Authentic faith cannot stay still—it
breathes through acts of love, showing the world the

living Christ within. Where faith has done its work in you, don't hold back your love from another, but let it overflow into the cup of another.

And now these three remain: faith, hope and love. But the greatest of these is love.

1 CORINTHIANS 13:13 NIV

UNITY AT THE EXPENSE OF THE WORLD

"Accursed be the love and the harmony for the preservation of which men endanger the Word of God."

There are times when peace must be sacrificed for truth. Luther's bold words remind us that not all "harmony" honors God. In a culture that prizes tolerance above conviction, it can be tempting to stay silent when Scripture is challenged or twisted. Yet love that ignores truth is no love at all, it's compromise disguised as kindness.

The Word of God is not fragile; it doesn't need our protection, but our courage to uphold it. Authentic peace flows from standing firm in what is right, not from blending in with what is wrong. When you must choose between comfort and conviction, remember: obedience to God's Word brings the only harmony that endures.

Even from your own number men will arise and distort the truth in order to draw away disciples after them. So be on your guard!

ACTS 20:30-31

DID YOU KNOW

There is no doubt that Luther was accused of dividing the Church for his criticisms of the Holy Roman Empire. However, his boldness unified fellow believers who shared his concerns. With the Edict of Worms in 1521, Lutheranism and largely Protestantism was born, beginning with Northern European bishops accepting his reforms.

FOUNDATIONAL DOCTRINES

"The litany of litanies is the Lord's Prayer. The learning of the learned is the Ten Commandments. The virtue of the virtuous is the Apostle's Creed . . . These three make a person perfect and absolute in thought, word, and deed; that is they nourish and bring to the highest perfection the mind, tongue, and body."

Luther saw great depth in the simplest truths of faith. The Ten Commandments guide our thoughts and choices; the Creed roots our words in truth; and the Lord's Prayer aligns our hearts with God's will. Together they form a rhythm of believing, speaking, and living that draws us closer to holiness.

In a world chasing spiritual novelty, the life of Luther shows us that holiness isn't found in new revelations, but in clinging to the timeless foundations of God's Word. His work as a reformer was not based on extra-biblical arguments of logic and intellect, but by holding up the plumb line of the Word of God to the practices of His Church.

Everything you need to spiritually thrive can be found in the foundation of the Bible. Sometimes, the most profound faith is simply remembering what we already know, and living it daily.

Finally, brethren, whatsoever things are
true, whatsoever things are honest,
whatsoever things are just, whatsoever
things are pure, whatsoever things are
lovely, whatsoever things are of good
report; if there be any virtue, and if there
be any praise, think on these things.

PHILIPPIANS 4:8

DON'T WAIT TO PRAY!

"Guard yourself carefully against those false, deluding ideas which tell you, Wait a little while. I will pray in an hour; first I must attend to this or that."

How easily distraction disguises itself as duty. *"I have to do this first,"* we tell ourselves. *"I'll pray later."* Yet, those small delays can be the enemy's quiet victories. Each postponed prayer hardens the heart a little more, until communion with God feels like a chore instead of a pleasure. When we neglect our prayer life, it can take time to rebuild the spiritual muscle memory.

Luther knew the truth: prayer is not something we fit into our life, it is what gives our life its shape. When we pause to seek God first, the rest of our day will find its proper order. Don't wait for the perfect time to pray; there isn't one. The perfect time is now, right where you are, because God is already listening.

"Therefore keep watch, because you do not know on what day your Lord will come. But understand this: If the owner of the house had known at what time of night the thief was coming, he would have kept watch and would not have let his house be broken into."

MATTHEW 24:42-43 NIV

DID YOU KNOW

In 1538, Luther wrote a hymnic version of the Lord's Prayer called *Vater unser im Himmelreich*. It was designed with a prayerful tune to function as both liturgy and a means of memorizing the scripture.

PEACE FROM HIS MERITS

"The way of peace is to believe without merits, nay, despite the greatest demerits simply to rely on the mercy of the Lord, just as the psalm bids us do: 'Cast thy burden upon the Lord.'"

A uthentic, lasting peace isn't found in self-improvement or moral perfection, it's found in surrender. The "way of peace" is not trying to earn it or achieve it, but trusting in the One who created everything and watches over everything.

Our hearts often carry the heavy burden of guilt and striving, whispering, *"I must do better."* All the while, Jesus walks beside you, wanting to lift the weight you are carrying. When we release our efforts to prove ourselves and rest in His unearned grace, peace is allowed to reign. Lay down your striving, your failures, and your pride. Let His mercy, not your merit, be the ground you stand on today.

"Cast thy burden upon the Lord, and he shall sustain thee: he shall never suffer the righteous to be moved."

PSALM 55:22

DID YOU KNOW

Luther's breakthrough on the mercy of God came during what is called his "*Tower Experience*," while studying Romans 1:17, when he realized that righteousness is not something we achieve, but something God gives through faith. This became the heart of his theology and the foundation for his teaching on peace through trusting God alone.

A HEALTHY FEAR

"Being afraid of God is different from fearing God. The fear of God is a fruit of love, but being afraid of Him is the seed of hatred."

Martin Luther draws a sharp yet beautiful distinction: being *afraid* of God drives us away, but *fearing* God draws us closer. To be afraid is to see God as a threat; to fear Him rightly is to stand in awe of His holiness, knowing His power is matched by His love.

The fear of God humbles us. It reminds us that we are small, yet deeply cherished. The same God who sent down plagues on Egypt also sent manna. The same Jesus who flipped tables and rebuked pharisees also multiplied food for the hungry and ate with sinners. It's the kind of fear that bows the knee, not in terror, but in reverence.

When we understand His goodness, fear transforms from dread into devotion. Let the love of God soften your heart today, so that your fear of Him becomes the fruit of trust, not the shadow of distance.

"The fear of the Lord is the beginning of knowledge: but fools despise wisdom and instruction."

PROVERBS 1:7

FAITH, NO DOUBT

*"We must constantly fight against doubt and unbelief,
so great and difficult a matter is faith."*

F aith is not a feeling we stumble upon, it's a daily battle we choose to fight. It's a discipline forged in the tension between trust and doubt. When the storms roll in, bills are overdue, and prayers appear unanswered, unbelief whispers that God has forgotten us. But a faith forged by fire, anchored in His promises, is what pulls us through.

Even the smallest act of trust, choosing to pray again, to open Scripture again, to hope again, is a victory. Faith grows not in the absence of doubt, but through the courage to resist it. Don't be discouraged if faith is not yet second-nature to you. Today, when unbelief knocks, answer with persistence: *"I will trust You still."* For in that simple stance, faith becomes strength.

"'If you can'?" said Jesus. "Everything is
possible for one who believes."
Immediately the boy's father exclaimed,
"I do believe; help me overcome my
unbelief!"

MARK 9:23-24 NIV

DID YOU KNOW

Luther's strong words against the Church and classism
stirred up long-festering radicalism among the poor in
Germany. Believing Luther supported their revolts, the
Great Peasant's War was waged between 1522-1525. While
Luther was initially sympathetic towards their grievances, he
quickly empasized that the *fight* he spoke of was a *spiritual*
one. Enraged by their burning of convents, monastaries,
libraries, and more, he condemned their violence as the
Devil's work.

WELCOMING DEATH

*"Christians look at [death] as a journey and departure out of
this misery and vale of tears (where the devil is prince and
god) into yonder life, where there will be inexpressible and
glorious joy and eternal blessedness."*

D eath, to the world, feels like an ending. The
mystery of what may or may not come
afterward has been a fear of humanity since
the beginning. But to the believer, as Luther wrote, it is
a journey and a passage from sorrow to everlasting joy.

Life on earth is marked by trials, tears, and temptation,
yet these are but shadows compared to the radiant glory
that awaits us in Christ. When fear of death grips us, we
can remember that we will be welcomed into the embrace
of the One who conquered the grave. For those in Christ,
death is not the end, but the beginning of a new adven-
ture. So we live not in dread, but in hope, knowing our
final destination is joy beyond imagining.

Since, then, you have been raised with
Christ, set your hearts on things above,
where Christ is, seated at the right hand
of God. Set your minds on things above,
not on earthly things.

COLOSSIANS 3:1-2 NIV

DID YOU KNOW

Because Luther's theology was centered on justification
by faith alone, he believed death had lost its power to
terrify the Christian. He acknowledged its pain and
uncertainty, especially as he lived through plagues, lost
two children, and suffered personal illness. Yet he often
described death as a "sleep" or a doorway from which
believers would awaken at the resurrection.

A BELIVER'S DUTY

"To serve God properly means that everyone stay in his calling, however humble it may be, and first heed the Word of God in church, then the word of the government, superiors, or parents, and then live accordingly."

There are many voices out there that claim they have the insight, the wisdom, the answer—all shouting and clamoring for your attention. One scroll through social media and you will find people saying you need this amount of money, this product, or this course to achieve happiness and success. But Martin Luther's words are a healthy reminder of the simplicity of our calling to godliness: serving with a humble heart.

To serve God properly means to bloom where you are planted, to honor Him in the role He's entrusted to you, however high or humble. Whether you're leading a company, teaching children, or caring for a home, your obedience in the small things is what reflects great devotion. God values the heart behind the work more than the size of the task. When we listen first to His Word, respect authority, and carry out our duties with integrity and joy, our everyday lives shine in a dark world.

Submit to one another out of reverence
for Christ.

EPHESIANS 5:21 NIV

UNJUST TO COMPLAIN

"It ill becomes a Christian to complain and clamor much about injustice done to him."

"I t's not fair!" Whether it's over sharing a toy, rationing Halloween candy, or a parent's discipline between quarreling siblings, these are the words every child utters at some point. This same attitude can carry out into adulthood when things don't go the way we imagined. It's natural to cry out against unfairness, but a heart anchored in Christ finds peace even in injustice.

Jesus Himself endured betrayal, mockery, and false accusations, yet *"opened not His mouth"* (Isaiah 53:7). When we follow His example, we show the world that our confidence rests not in human fairness, but in God's perfect justice. Complaining deepens bitterness, while silence opens the door for His vindication. For the humble heart, every injustice becomes an invitation to trust Him more deeply, to reflect His grace instead of resentment, and find a godly resolution. Surrender the outcome to the One who always judges righteously, and peace will be yours.

"The Lord shall fight for you, and ye shall hold your peace."

EXODUS 14:14

FUSSING OR HAVING FAITH?

"We should not become impatient but should learn to watch, wait, and continue steadfast in faith; for we see what people are like when they become impatient, how they fuss and fume and carry on. They only hinder their own praying and praising."

I mpatience is one of faith's quietest enemies. When we grow restless waiting on God, our worry can choke our worship. We start to "fuss and fume," thinking our timing is better than His. But faith is not proved in answered prayers, it's proved in the waiting.

When we trust that God is still working behind the scenes, our hearts find peace in His promises rather than our schedules. Like a farmer who plants and then patiently tends the soil, we must learn to rest in the unseen growth of God's will.

Waiting is not wasted time. It is sacred space where trust deepens, we mature in our devotion, and our prayers are purified into simple, steady faith.

A person's wisdom yields patience;
it is to one's glory to overlook an offense.

PROVERBS 19:11 NIV

DID YOU KNOW

Luther learned the lesson of patience well during his
nearly year-long period of hiding in Wartburg Castle
after being declared an outlaw. Cut off from public
ministry and unable to preach or lead the reform
openly, Luther was forced into a season of watching,
waiting, and enduring uncertainty. He referred to this
time as "*my Patmos*".

PRACTICE YOUR PREACHING

"God grants us all to live as we teach and to practice what we preach."

W hen you receive a serious diagnosis from your doctor, choosing faith over fear is no small task. Choosing to bite your tongue and be humble in the face of criticism can feel like an internal battle. Taking the high road or turning the other cheek when you've been wronged can take every fiber of your strength. It's easy to speak of faith, love, and humility, but much harder to live them daily.

Faith is not proven in eloquent speech, but in quiet consistency. It's found in forgiving when it's hard, serving when it's inconvenient, and standing firm when compromise feels easier. The world doesn't need more talk; it needs living examples. Our daily lives lived in simple faith are our greatest witness to the world.

Ask God to align your heart with your words so that your life becomes a living sermon of grace, truth, and love that points others toward Him.

Dear children, let us not love with words or speech but with actions and in truth.

1 JOHN 3:18 NIV

CARELESS WORK

"We should indeed work, but we should let God have the care. After all, our worrying gets us nowhere. Meanwhile we might have done much good, but our care has kept us from it."

How times have you gone about your work, taking calls or tackling chores, all the while wading through anxious thoughts? *How can I mend this relationship? How will I pay this bill? How can I get through this seemingly endless list of tasks?* When we spend our days tangled in anxiety, wondering if things will turn out right, we rob ourselves of the joy and peace that come from trusting God.

Worry is like quicksand. The more you strive in your own strength, the deeper you sink. When we still our hearts and trust God, we can grab hold of the rope of His grace that pulls us out of the pit. Faith releases our struggle for control and lets God carry the burden that was never ours to bear.

Today, as you go about your work, pause and ask yourself: *am I holding onto the lifeline God has thrown me or am I trying to prove I can do it all on my own?* Lift your heart to God and let His peace fill the space where anxiety once lived.

"Casting all your care upon him; for he careth for you."

1 PETER 5:7

RIGHT DOCTRINE ESSENTIAL

"It is true, where the doctrine is not right, it is impossible for the life to be right and good; for life is fathered and fashioned by doctrine."

Wﾠhat we truly believe inevitably shapes how we live. Doctrine isn't an abstract set of ideas tucked away in dusty books, it is the foundation that forms our choices, our attitudes, and our character.

When our understanding of God is distorted, our lives wobble with it. When our hearts are anchored in truth, our steps become steady and intentional. Strong doctrine leads us to see God rightly, ourselves honestly, and the world clearly. It corrects, comforts, and realigns us with His heart.

When we make God's truth our pursuit and submit to it, we stand out in a world inundated with hurting people searching for purpose. Let His truth reshape any crooked places in your heart, so your life may become a living testimony of the truth that gives it strength.

"The entrance of thy words giveth light; it giveth understanding unto the simple."

PSALM 119:130

DO NOT CRUSH A CHILD

"Children are not to be rebuked or beaten, but that they are to be chastised in love; but parents are not to vent their furious temper on them . . . For when the spirit has been cowed, one is of no use for anything."

L uther's words are a reminder that correction is meant to shape, not break. Children thrive under guidance rooted in patient love, not in an environment where love is a transaction based on performance. Discipline given in anger may force outward obedience and results, but it crushes the spirit and stifles trust, confidence, and joy.

God, our loving Father, never disciplines us out of rage. His correction is measured, purposeful, and always centered around restoration. He may lead us through hard seasons and difficult roads, but His promise is that He is always beside us. When we mirror His heart, our words become gentler, our tone calmer, and our reactions wiser.

Whether you are raising a child, mentoring someone younger, or even correcting yourself, remember: discipline without love wounds, but love with intention heals.

"And fathers, do not provoke your children to anger; but bring them up in the discipline and instruction of the Lord."

EPHESIANS 6:4 NASB

CHOOSING A WIFE

"Ask God to give you a good, pious girl, with whom you spend your life in mutual love. For sex [alone] establishes nothing . . . there must also be agreement in values and character."

Caleb thought he knew what he wanted in a wife—someone beautiful, adventurous, and exciting. But after a string of shallow relationships, he found himself more lonely than ever. One Saturday morning, he had breakfast with his grandfather and vented his relationship woes. His grandfather shared this wisdom with him: while he found his wife was beautiful, it was her character he observed over a year of friendship that convinced him she was the one for him. They held similar values, they complemented each other, and where they differed only spurred him on to grow as a man.

Caleb began praying differently. Instead of allowing

his eyes to lead the way, he asked for integrity, kindness, and shared devotion. Months later, he met Anna, a woman whose gentle strength and faith steadied him. Their connection grew not from sparks alone, but from shared vision and mutual love. Luther's wisdom rang true in Caleb's heart: lasting love is built on character, not chemistry.

"Can two walk together, except they be agreed?"

AMOS 3:3

ANGELS AT OUR SIDE

"You should be certain that angels are protecting you when you go to sleep, yea, that they are protecting you also in all your business, whether you enter your home or leave your home."

Martin Luther's statement reminds us of a truth we often forget: we are never unguarded. Scripture assures us that God *"commands His angels concerning you"*, not just in moments of danger, but in the ordinary rhythm of life. When you lock your door at night, when you drive to work, when you step into another uncertain day, you do so under divine watch.

If we could see what God shields us from, there is no doubt our hearts would overflow with gratitude. When you lay your head down to sleep tonight, breathe deeply and rest. The God who loves you has assigned His angels to stand guard.

"Are not all angels ministering spirits sent
to serve those who will inherit salvation?"

HEBREWS 1:14 NIV

DID YOU KNOW

While Luther spoke extensively on devils, he was also a firm
believer in angels. He wrote: "The angels are near to us, to
those creatures whom by God's command they are to
preserve, to the end we receive no hurt of the devil . . . the
loving holy angels resist and drive him away; for the angels
have long arms, and although they stand before the face and
in the presence of God and his son Christ, yet they are hard
by and about us in those affairs, which by God we are
commanded to take in hand."

WHERE THERE IS SMOKE

*"Just as there is no fire without heat and smoke,
so there is no faith without love."*

The moment a sinner repents and accepts Christ, a match strikes and a flame is born in the heart of the new believer. Joy and gratitude are the kindling God breathes His love into. As the fire grows, it radiates the same warmth of the Creator as a natural overflow of a heart transformed by grace.

When God transforms you inwardly, the changes become apparent outwardly. Your fire becomes a source of comfort and guidance in a cold world, drawing those wandering in the darkness nearer to the source of warmth. Your patience grows deeper, your kindness stretches further, and your compassion becomes more instinctive.

If your faith feels cold today, don't try to manufacture love. Draw near again to God, rekindle your trust in Him, and love will follow as surely as warmth follows fire. Authentic faith burns bright and authentic love rises with it.

If I have the gift of prophecy and can fathom all mysteries and all knowledge, and if I have a faith that can move mountains, but do not have love, I am nothing.

1 CORINTHIANS 13:2 NIV

OVERCOMING CIRCUMSTANCES

"If I really recognize my blessings, my heart laughs; and if He sends me misfortune, trouble, and danger, I take to thanking Him and say: God be forever praised for chastising me in this way."

L uther's words invite us into a deeper gratitude—one that doesn't depend on circumstances but on trust in God's wisdom. When
we fully recognize our blessings, joy manifests. Our
hearts "laugh" because we see God's kindness in every
good thing.

But Luther challenges us even further: to thank
God even in misfortune, trouble, and danger. Not because
pain is pleasant, but because our Father never wastes
it. Trials and tribulations shape us, strengthen us, and
are opportunities to draw closer to Him. God's goodness bridges the gap when we can't see the way to joy
in dark times.

When difficulties come, instead of asking, "Why me?" we can whisper, "What are You forming in me?" Gratitude shifts the battle. Praise in hardship softens the heart, deepens faith, and reminds us that signs of God's unwavering love are abundant even in the storm.

"I have learned the secret of being content in any and every situation, whether well fed or hungry, whether living in plenty or in want."

PHILIPPIANS 4:12 NIV

LIFE'S UPS AND DOWNS

"How is God to arrange our life? Good days we cannot bear; evil days we cannot endure. If He gives us wealth, we strut about; if He gives us poverty, we despair. It would be best to hurry us under ground with the spade."

How easily our hearts can swing between pride and despair on the tightrope of life. When life is good, we often take credit and call ourselves "self-made", forgetting the Giver. When life is hard, we crumble and complain, forgetting His nearness.

God sees this instability and lovingly calls us back to a steadier center: Himself. We weren't made to stand alone in our own strength. On the tightrope of life, we were made to be dependent on God to maintain the balance between humility and confidence, grace and discipline. He knows exactly what we need because He has known us from our very beginning. He knows what shapes us, humbles us, strengthens us, and draws us closer to Him.

Instead of praying for easier days, let's ask for a steadier heart that praises in abundance and trusts in scarcity.

Rejoice always, pray continually, give thanks in all circumstances; for this is God's will for you in Christ Jesus.

1 THESSALONIANS 5:16-18 NIV

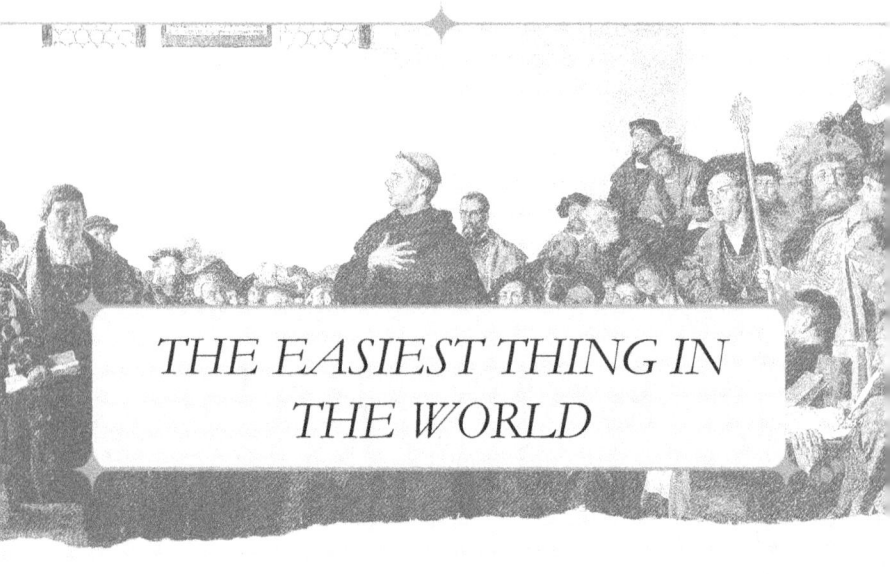

THE EASIEST THING IN
THE WORLD

"Nothing is easier than sinning."

I t takes no effort at all to slip into impatience, self-centeredness, careless words, or compromise. Sin doesn't need to be taught, it begins to manifest early in the impatience of a child or the unwillingness to share a toy and grows from there. Sin flows with the natural current of the human heart.

But the ease of sin is exactly what makes grace so stunning. God does not abandon us to our weakness, but He meets us in it. When we drift, the Holy Spirit doesn't shame us, but serves as the gentle whisper of truth and conviction that guides us back to the path.

Each act of obedience, however small or unseen, becomes a reminder that Christ's power is at work within us. And when we fail—and we will—grace calls us back, lifts our chin, and points us toward better things. Resist the sinful nature today and put on your true identity in Christ. Cling to the One who makes holiness possible, even for hearts that wander.

For I know that good itself does not dwell in me, that is, in my sinful nature. For I have the desire to do what is good, but I cannot carry it out. For I do not do the good I want to do, but the evil I do not want to do—this I keep on doing.

ROMANS 7:18-19 NIV

COMFORTED BEYOND
OUR SENSES

"The comfort men give consists in external, visible help, which one can grasp, see, and feel. The comfort God gives consists only in the Word and promise, without seeing, hearing, or feeling."

Human comfort is often limited to tangible means; helping hands, warm words, and visible solutions. And these gifts matter. But God's comfort is of a different kind. It anchors us not in what we can see, but in what He has spoken. When circumstances offer no evidence of hope, His promises stand unchanged. When feelings mislead us, His Word brings us back to truth. Where friends fall short, God is forever faithful. His Spirit ministers to our spirit, and the work that is done transcends flesh and soothes the soul. This is the comfort that carries us through nights when nothing seems to help and no human rationale can solve what we are going through.

Faith grows strong in those unseen places, clinging to the God who cannot lie. Let His promises be your steady ground. Choose to rest not in what your eyes observe, but in what His Word has declared.

Yea, though I walk through the valley of
the shadow of death, I will fear no evil:
for thou art with me; thy rod and thy staff
they comfort me.

PSALM 23:4

TRIALS ARE BENEFICIAL

"One Christian who has been tried is worth a hundred who have not been tried, for the blessing of God grows in trials. He who has experienced them can teach, comfort, and advise many in bodily and spiritual matters."

Trials do more than test us, they transform us. A believer who has walked through fire carries a depth that cannot be learned from books or sermons. In hardship, God stretches our faith, deepens our compassion, and sharpens our wisdom. What once felt like brokenness becomes, in time, a blessing we can pass on. Those who have been hurt understand healing, those who have been afraid know how to seek peace, and those who have waited know how to cultivate patience.

If you are facing hardship today, take heart: God can use everything for good. Your story, refined by His grace, could one day become someone else's lifeline.

Consider it pure joy, my brothers and
sisters, whenever you face trials of many
kinds, because you know that the testing
of your faith produces perseverance.

JAMES 1:2-3

DID YOU KNOW

While we know well how Luther endured trials of
persecution for his faith and convictions, he was no stranger
to physical illness. From 1531 until his death in 1546, he
began to suffer with kidney stones, arthritis, and vertigo,
fainting, and tinnitus caused by a ruptured ear drum. His
poor health contributed to his short temper, producing some
of his harshest and most controversial writing in these final
years. Ultimately, he passed away after a stroke at the age of 62.

THE HOLY SPIRIT'S BEST SELLER

"The Bible is the special, very own Book, Writing, and Word of the Holy Spirit."

L uther's statement calls us to remember that Scripture is not merely ancient ink on old pages, but the very breath of God preserved for us. The Bible carries a life and authority no other book possesses because its Author still speaks through every line. When you open it, you are not simply reading ink on paper—you are meeting God, receiving wisdom crafted for your steps, healing for your wounds, and truth to keep your paths straight. Yet how often do we overlook this treasure, treating it as ordinary?

Today, approach Scripture with fresh reverence. Ask the Spirit who wove it together to illuminate it again, so its power doesn't stay on the page but sinks into your heart.

All Scripture is God-breathed and is useful for teaching, rebuking, correcting and training in righteousness, so that the servant of God may be thoroughly equipped for every good work.

2 TIMOTHY 3:16-17 NIV

DID YOU KNOW

The printing press was invented in 1440 by Johannes Gutenberg, who combined technology in woodblock printing and ink development with the ancient Roman screw press, and mechanized both Chinese and Islamic paper making techniques. By making the printed word more accessible, Luther's writings spread significantly more widely than they could have before it's timely invention.

BLESSED DEPARTURE

"The hour of our death is a heavenly gift for which we should constantly ask God and daily prepare ourselves so that . . . we look forward to our departure and our gain with pious longing."

D aniel had feared death since he was a child. He lost his mother to cancer at a young age, which formed an anxious avoidance of hospitals and funerals.

In her final days, she spoke of heaven with a sparkle in her eyes, as if she were packing for a long-awaited trip. Her peace disturbed him as a child—why didn't she fight harder? Why was she so eager to leave him behind?

Daniel grew older and eventually came into his own faith in God. With time and the Holy Spirit's healing, he began to understand his mother's peace. He realized that death for the believer is not an end, but a homecoming. She was waiting patiently for him on the other side. He felt his own fear slowly uncoil.

Now he prays not out of fear of death, but to be ready; living each day with gratitude, trust, and expectation for the moment Christ calls him safely home.

"For me to live is Christ and die is gain."

PHILIPPIANS 1:21 NIV

THE BURDEN OF
PROSPERITY

*"When things are going well, a man cannot control himself by
means of his own powers; he becomes presumptuous, prides
himself on his wealth and good fortune, and passes away."*

When life is smooth and blessings stack
up like unopened gifts, it's tempting to
believe we're the ones steering the ship.
Our hearts can so easily drift into pride, assuming our
strength, strategy, or success built the life we enjoy.
But prosperity in and of itself is a poor teacher whose
lessons are easily forgotten. How quickly we can forget
where we came from and who helped us get there.

Scripture reminds us that every good and perfect
gift comes from above, not from our own hands. Instead
of letting abundance make us mindlessly arrogant, we
can let it make us exceedingly grateful. When blessings
come, pause and acknowledge the Giver. Keep your

eyes open for opportunities to aid those who stand where you once stood. Let success deepen humility, not diminish it. The moment we operate as if we don't need God is the moment we make gods of ourselves. Security comes not from fortune but from the One who never slumbers.

Believers in humble circumstances ought to take pride in their high position. But the rich should take pride in their humiliation—since they will pass away like a wild flower.

JAMES 1:9-10 NIV

THE ONGOING ARGUMENT

*"Think of all the squabbles Adam and Eve must have had
in the course of their nine hundred years. Eve would say, 'You
ate the apple,' and Adam would retort, 'You gave it to me.'"*

Martin Luther brings humor to a timeless
truth: human conflict is nothing new.
The blame game is played regularly by
stubborn children and couples alike. If Adam and
Eve—who walked with God in the garden—could bicker
for centuries over blame, how much more are we prone
to defend ourselves and point fingers? Yet their story
also reminds us of something deeper: even after the
fall, God did not abandon them. He did not see them
as a failed creation to throw into the bin and start over,
but He clothed them, guided them, and stayed with
them and their descendants to this very day.

When tension rises in our own relationships, instead

of dwelling on who "started it," we can invite grace into the conversation. God is present not only in our harmony, but also in our mess. And where His grace enters, healing begins.

... for all have sinned and fall short of the glory of God, and all are justified freely by his grace through the redemption that came by Christ Jesus.

ROMANS 3:23-24 NIV

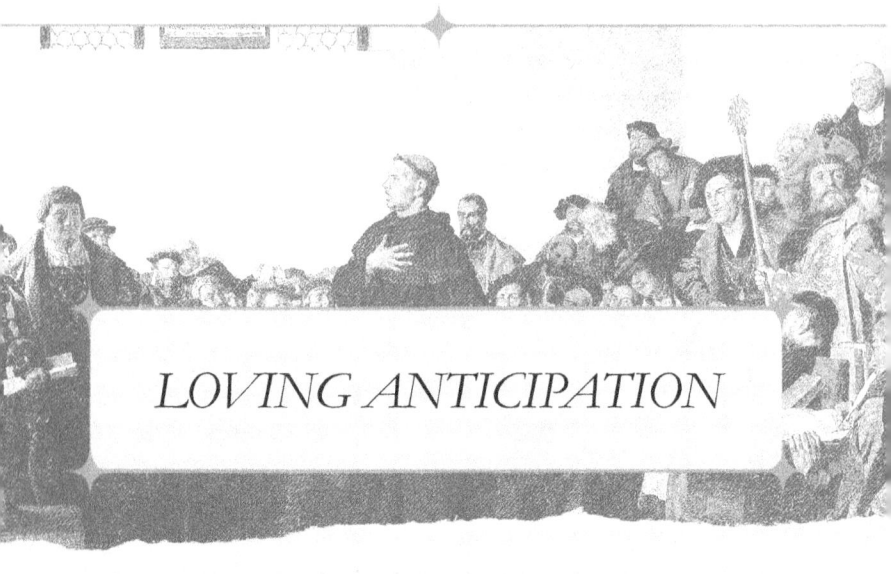

LOVING ANTICIPATION

"Let the wife make her husband glad to come home and let him make her sorry he leaves."

E van and Mara had found themselves settled in uneasy rhythm of life. Mara felt overwhelmed with the life of a a stay-at-home mom and Evan craved respite from the pressure of working and providing. Over years, they neglected each other's needs and as the gap between them grew wider, they began to resent each other for it.

It all came out in a blowout argument on a weeknight. After the shouting subsided, they both sat quietly, realizing something needed to change. The next morning, Evan got up with the kids so Mara could sleep in, and surprised her with breakfast already made. With the extra energy fueling her day, Mara maneuvered through the day with more ease. Evan arrived home to a clean house and a hot meal, with Mara ushering him in to sit, eat, and relax after a long day.

Day by day, small choices softened old patterns. He began lingering a little longer before work; she found herself smiling when she heard his key in the door. They realized love grows not from grand gestures but from daily decisions to bless one another. In choosing kindness, they rediscovered joy and each other.

Be completely humble and gentle; be patient, bearing with one another in love. Make every effort to keep the unity of the Spirit through the bond of peace.

EPHESIANS 4:2-3 NIV

TWO THINGS ALONE

*"Every man must do two things alone; he must do his own
believing and his own dying."*

This is a truth known well by Christian parents across the world who strive to raise Christian children: ultimately you cannot force faith. Faith cannot be borrowed or inherited; it must be personally embraced, wrestled with, and rooted in the heart. Others can encourage us, educate us, pray for us, and point us toward Christ, but in the end we must choose for ourselves to trust the Savior who gave everything for us. We can memorize verses, attend all the Christian clubs or study groups, and say all the right words, but we must take interest in a personal relationship with God.

Just as no one can believe on our behalf, no one can

face eternity in our place. Yet here is our great comfort: though we walk these paths alone, we do not walk them *without God*. Christ meets us in our believing with grace, and He will meet us in our dying with glory. Live today in that holy assurance.

So then every one of us shall give account of himself to God.

ROMANS 14:12

RANKS OF THE ENEMY

"They are small devils that tempt with lasciviousness and avarice; higher spirits tempt with unbelief, and despair, and heresy."

Not all battles of the soul look the same. Some temptations are obvious—lust, greed, selfish desire—but these, he says, are "small devils." They are tangible sins that arise naturally from our flesh without much influence from others.

The greater dangers are subtle and far more destructive: unbelief that whispers God is distant, despair that convinces us hope is gone, and false teaching that leads us away from truth. These may not set off alarm bells in the beginning, but they slowly erode your faith and your perception of God. Yet Scripture assures us that Christ is greater than every spiritual foe, the Holy Spirit equips us to discern, and we are joined to a body of fellow believers that watches out for us. When doubts rise, cling to God's Word. When despair presses in, speak His promises aloud or reach out to a brother or sister. When confusion comes, return to the simplicity of the gospel.

For we wrestle not against flesh and blood, but against principalities, against powers, against the rulers of the darkness of this world, against spiritual wickedness in high places.

EPHESIANS 6:12

SPRING RISES AGAIN

"Our Lord has written the promise of the resurrection, not in books alone, but in every leaf of springtime."

For most of humanity's history, winter has been a harsh and deadly season. It's only in recent centuries that we benefit from advances in civilization by cozying up in our homes with a hot drink on cold days. But even with our modern creature comforts, we still feel the effects of cold and reduced sun exposure that can make winter a struggle. Observing the "death" of nature during winter can illicit depressive thoughts, but with a deeper look we see why winter is essential to the bursting life of spring.

Snowfall insulates plants and animals for the season, and lets water soak deep into the soil. Cold stratification is the process of exposing seeds to cold and moist conditions that boosts or is often even required for germination in spring. Cold temperatures also keep pest populations in check.

There is a time and purpose for every season. If you find yourself in a wintry season, consider this wisdom built into in God's creation and trust that spring is coming.

For since the creation of the world God's invisible qualities—his eternal power and divine nature—have been clearly seen, being understood from what has been made, so that people are without excuse.

ROMANS 1:20 NIV

PRAYER STOKES THE FIRE

"If I should neglect prayer but a single day, I should lose a great deal of the fire of faith."

Martin Luther understood something we often feel but rarely are humble enough to admit: our faith cools quickly when prayer grows sparse. It isn't that God withdraws, but it's our hearts that drift either by distraction or delusion of independence. Prayer keeps us near the flame, warming us with His presence, lighting our path ahead, and softening the places that grow rigid with worry or pride.

When we neglect prayer, even for a day, our thoughts scatter, our peace wavers, and our trust feels fragile. Our spiritual cogs grow rusty and don't function at their best. But the beauty of God's mercy is that the fire can be stirred again—any moment, any time. A whispered "Lord, I'm here" is enough to rekindle the embers. Today, return to Him in simple prayer. Don't get hung up on what you should say or how long you should pray. Let His nearness reignite your faith.

Be joyful in hope, patient in affliction,
faithful in prayer.

ROMANS 12:12 NIV

PRAYER, OUR LIFEBLOOD

"To be a Christian without prayer is no more possible than to be alive without breathing."

J ust as a body weakens without oxygen, our spirits wither when prayer slips to the margins. Like any relationship, effort is required to connect and have conversation with one another. Prayer is no exception, but the beauty of it is that you don't need to coordinate schedules or travel to meet God— you can engage with God anywhere and anytime.

Whether it's a prayer whispered under your breath in the flurry of family life, a quiet moment between serving customers, or utilizing your commute, there is always time in your day to spend with God. It's not about perfect words or long sessions, it's about staying connected to the One who gives life.

When we breathe in His presence through prayer, we exhale worry, fear, and self-reliance. As we learn to make prayer our rhythm, our spirits grow stronger, steadier, and more alive. Today, breathe deep, talk to God, and let Him meet you with grace.

Devote yourselves to prayer, being
watchful and thankful.

COLOSSIANS 4:2

THE FOOLS WHO
ARE WISE

*"It is characteristic of a Christian to have the greatest strength
in the greatest weakness and the greatest wisdom in the
greatest foolishness."*

G od often works in ways that look upside-down to the world, even foolish or non-sensical. Think of Gideon in the book of Judges. When preparing to attack the Midianites who were threatening Israel, God repeatedly told Gideon to reduce his armies until there were only three hundred left. Against all logic and military strategy, God delivered them into their hands.

The story of Gideon teaches us that our greatest strength isn't found in our confidence or capability, but in our trust and obedience. It's in our weakness that God's power shines brightest. And the wisdom He gives doesn't always appear impressive. Sometimes it's choosing kindness when a harsh word would feel warranted, or trusting God when logic says to panic. Yet these "foolish" choices rooted in faith carry divine wisdom that transforms us and those around us.

When life exposes your limits, don't be discouraged. In your smallest, most fragile moments, you are never stronger or wiser than when you lean wholly on Him.

"For when I am weak, then I am strong."

2 CORINTHIANS 12:10 NIV

GOD LOVES LAUGHTER

*"It is pleasing to God whenever you rejoice or laugh from the
bottom of your heart."*

As we go through daily life, striving to live
righteously and denying our fleshy tenden-
cies, we can fall into a rut of self-deprecat-
ing legalism if we aren't careful. Legalism says there
is always something you need to do better to earn
God's love, keeping you bogged down by picking apart
every fault and forgetting God's grace. But God does
not take pleasure in our self-inflicted, needless misery
we disguise as piousness.

A good father delights in the joy of his children.
When you laugh freely, when your heart feels light,
when gratitude bubbles up unexpectedly, God delights
in it. Joy is often treated as optional in a world that

prizes productivity and seriousness, but Scripture paints it as a fruit of the Spirit, a sign that God is near. Your joy is not a denial of life's hardships, but it is a declaration that God is bigger than them.

Let your heart laugh today at a small blessing, a good joke, or a glimpse of God's goodness. Every sincere moment of joy is shared by heaven.

Even though you do not see him now, you are filled with an inexpressible and glorious joy.

1 PETER 1:8 NIV

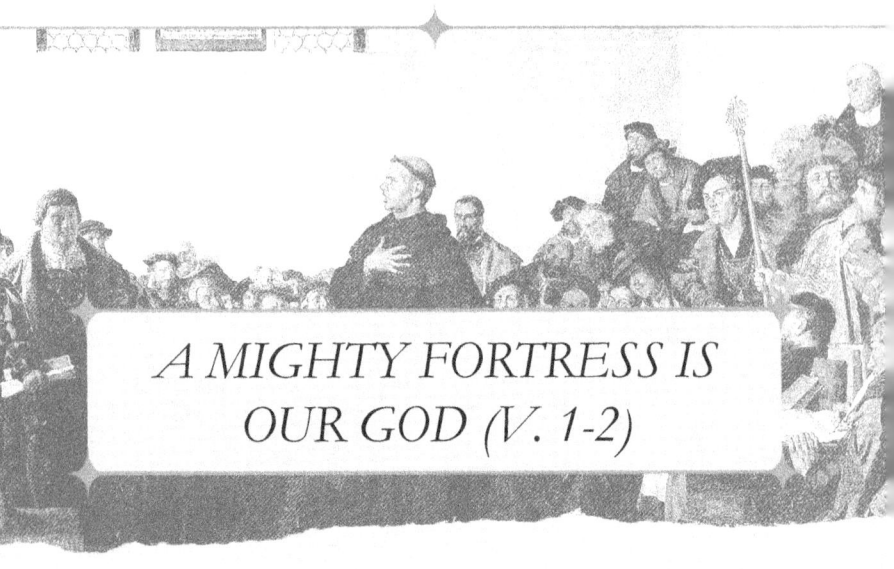

A MIGHTY FORTRESS IS OUR GOD (V. 1-2)

A Mighty Fortress Is Our God, titled "Ein feste Burg ist unser Gott" in German, is a hymn composed by Martin Luther in 1529.

A mighty fortress is our God,
    A bulwark never failing;
Our helper He, amid the flood
Of mortal ills prevailing.
For still our ancient foe
Doth seek to work us woe;
His craft and power are great,
And, armed with cruel hate,
On earth is not his equal.

D id we in our own strength confide,
Our striving would be losing,
Were not the right Man on our side,
The Man of God's own choosing.
Dost ask who that may be?
Christ Jesus, it is He;
Lord Sabaoth His name,
From age to age the same,
And He must win the battle.

The Lord is my rock, and my fortress, and
my deliverer; my God, my strength, in
whom I will trust; my buckler, and the
horn of my salvation, and my high tower.

PSALM 18:2

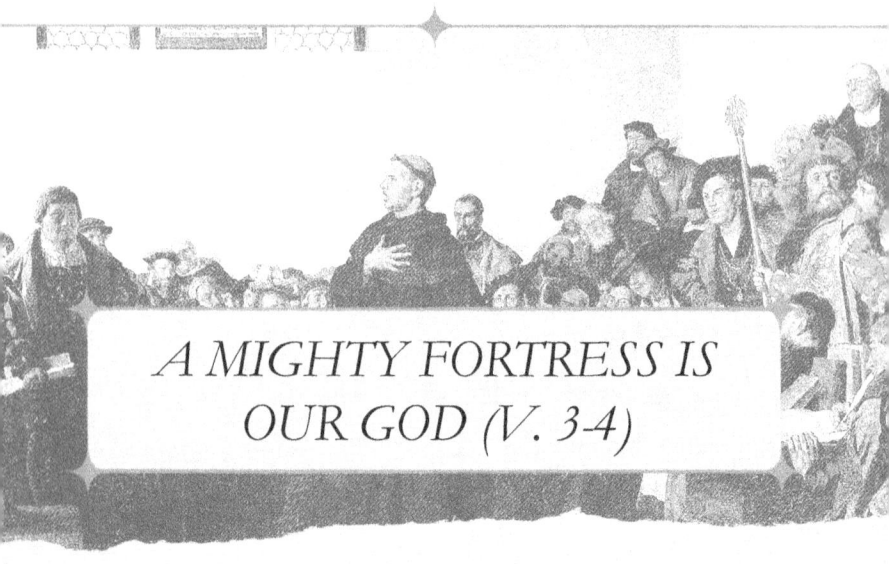

A MIGHTY FORTRESS IS OUR GOD (V. 3-4)

A Mighty Fortress Is Our God, titled "Ein feste Burg ist unser Gott" in German, is a hymn composed by Martin Luther in 1529.

And though this world, with devils filled,
　　　Should threaten to undo us,
We will not fear, for God hath willed
His truth to triumph through us.
The prince of darkness grim
We tremble not for him;
His rage we can endure,
For lo! His doom is sure,
One little word shall fell him.

That word above all earthly powers
No thanks to them abideth;
The Spirit and the gifts are ours
Through Him who with us sideth.
Let goods and kindred go,
This mortal life also;
The body they may kill:
God's truth abideth still,
His kingdom is forever.

I pray that the eyes of your heart may be enlightened in order that you may know the hope to which he has called you, the riches of his glorious inheritance in his holy people, and his incomparably great power for us who believe.

EPHESIANS 1:18-19

If you have enjoyed this book, look out for these other additions to the series for sale online:

D. L. Moody's Little Instruction Book

John Wesleys's Little Instruction Book

Martin Luther's Little Instruction Book

C. S. Lewis's Little Instruction Book

Charles Spurgeon's Little Instruction Book

A. W. Tozer's Little Instruction Book

If this book has impacted your life, we would love to hear from you.

Please contact us at info@honorbooks.com